FROM THE FILMS OF

Harry Potter

AN OFFICIAL
HOGWARTS
COLORING BOOK

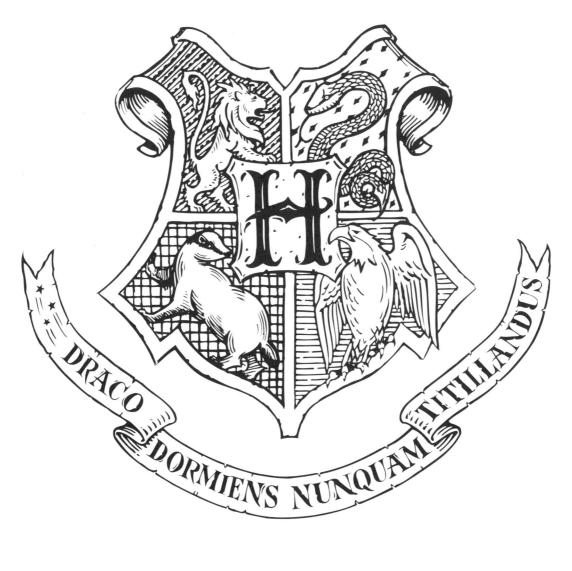

INSIGHT
EDITIONS

SAN RAFAEL • LOS ANGELES • LONDON

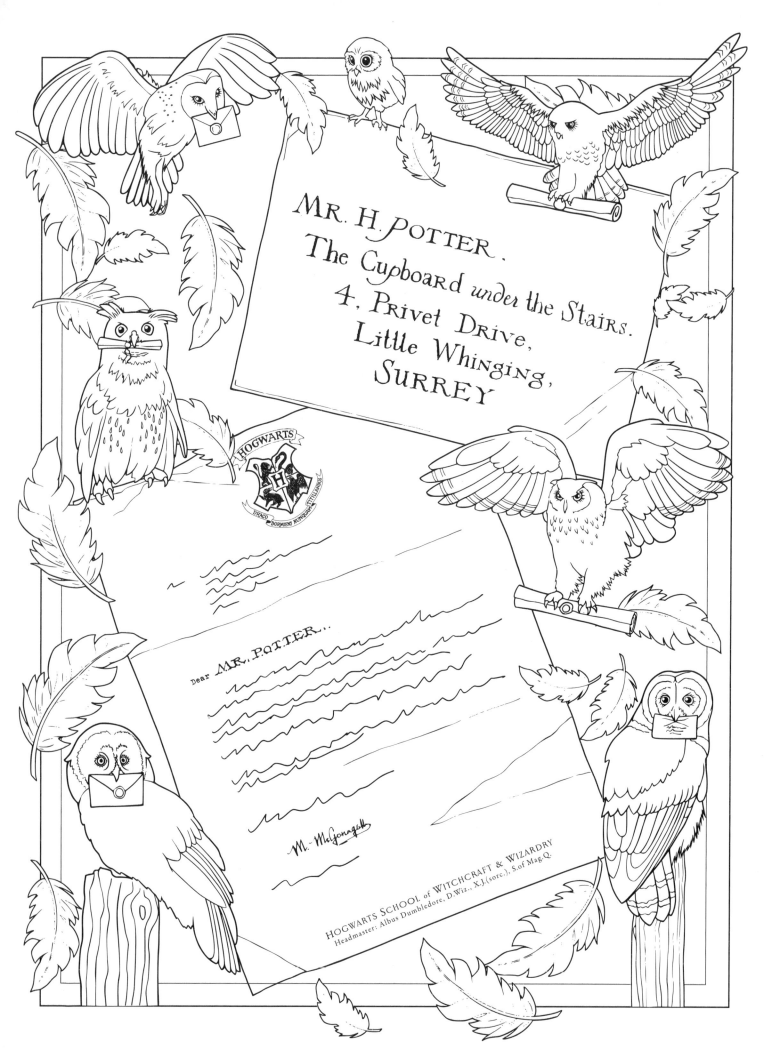

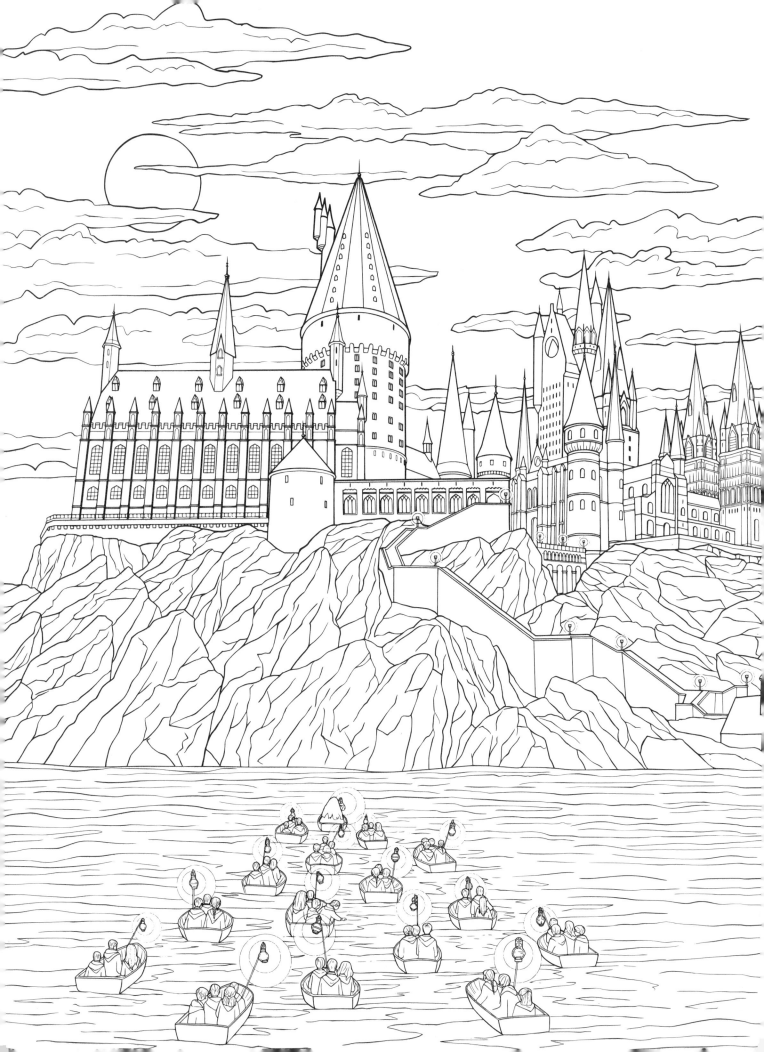

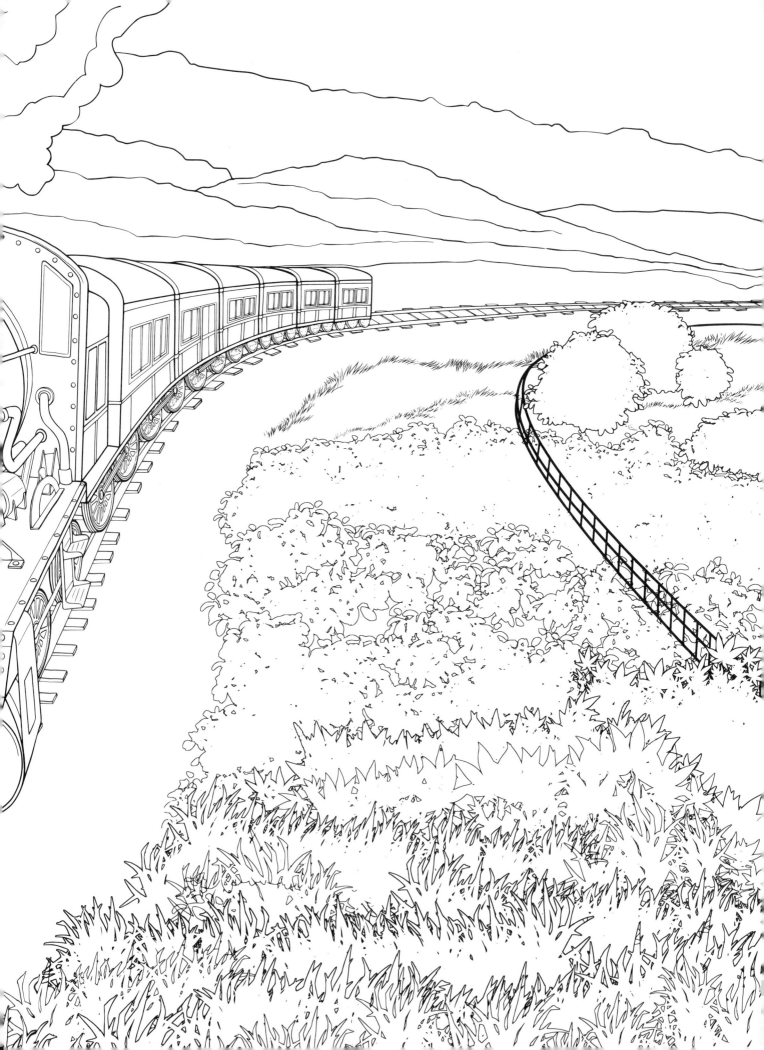

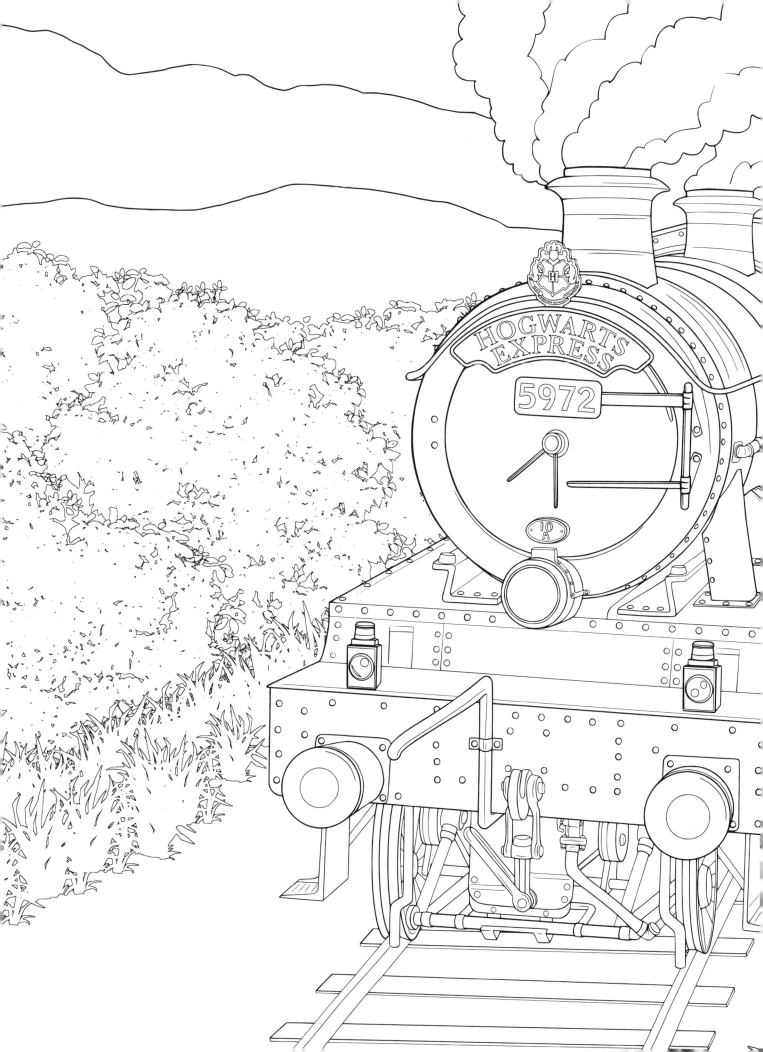

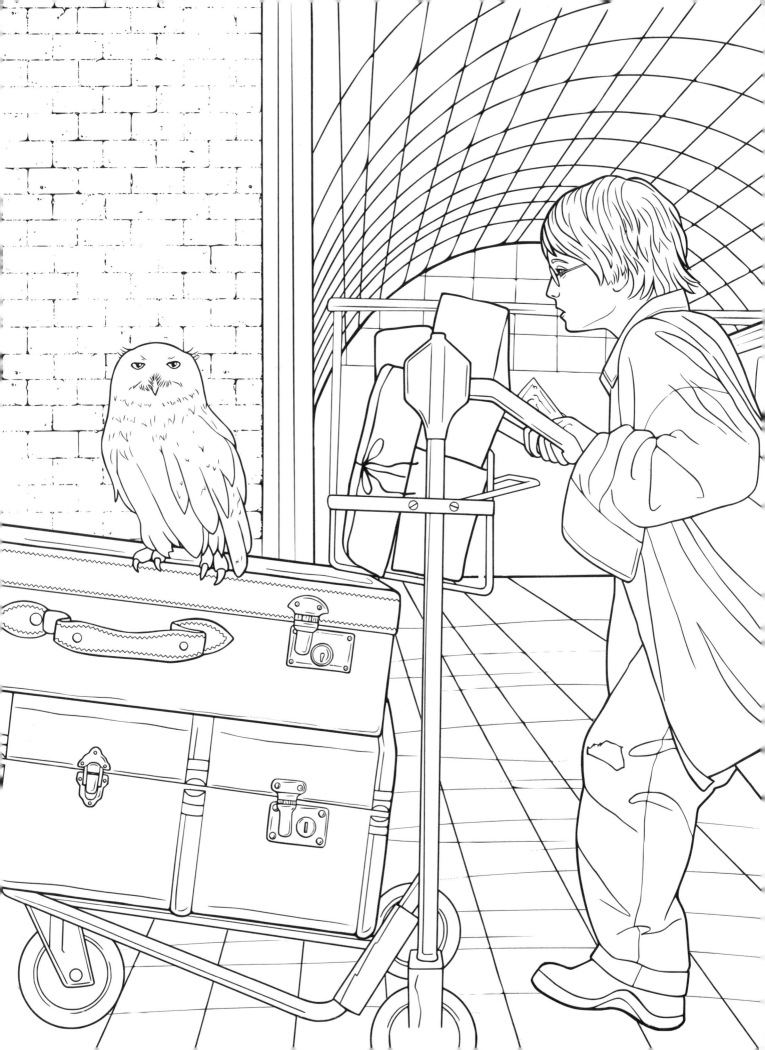

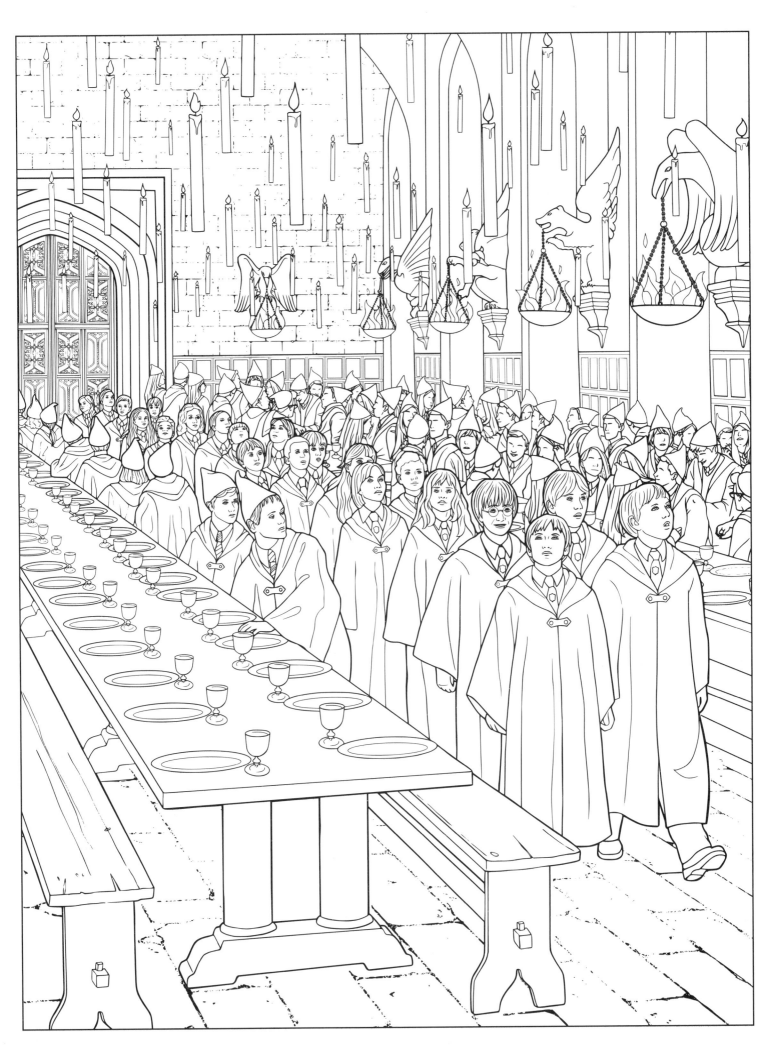

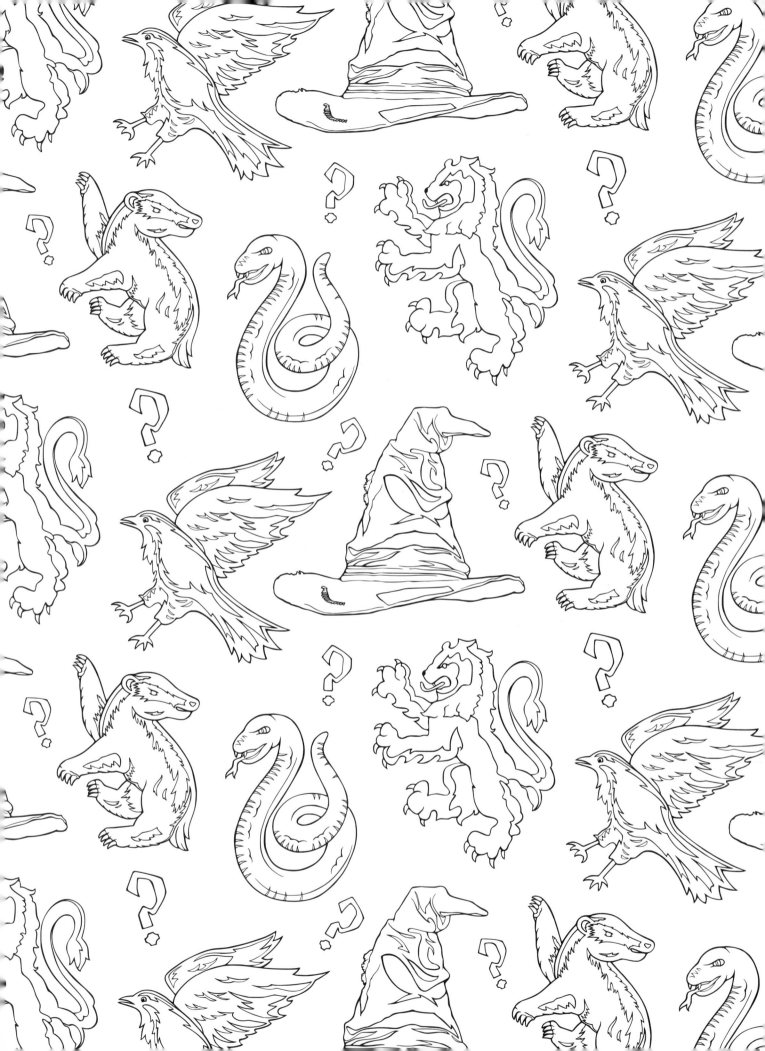

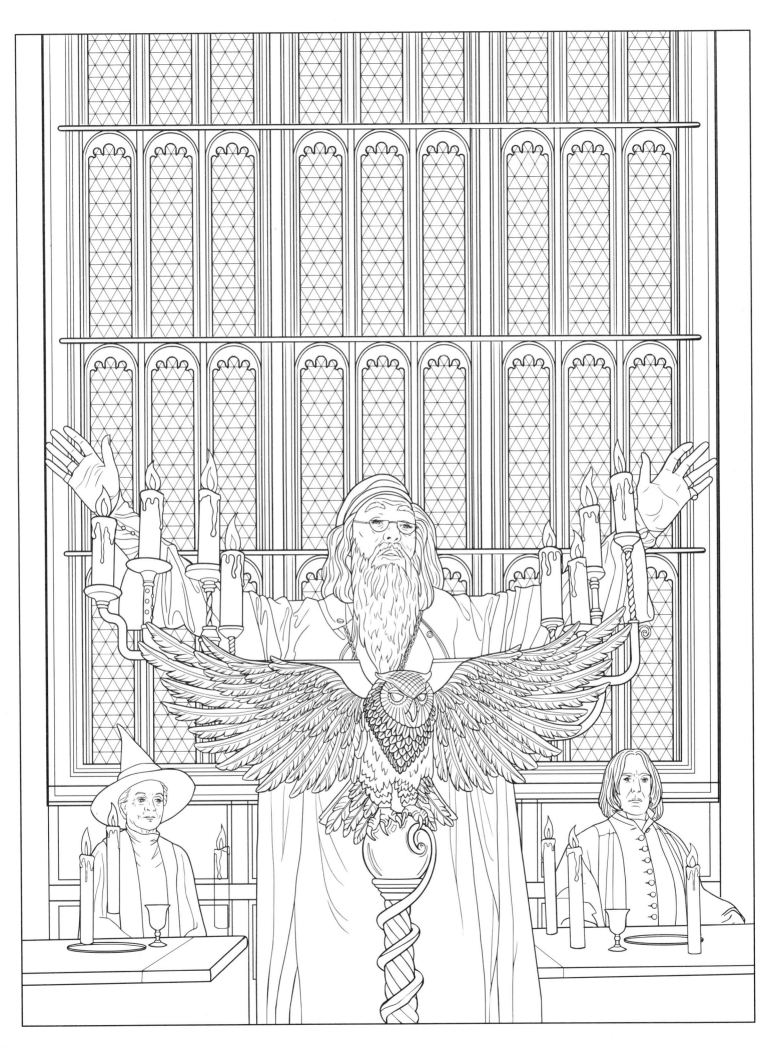

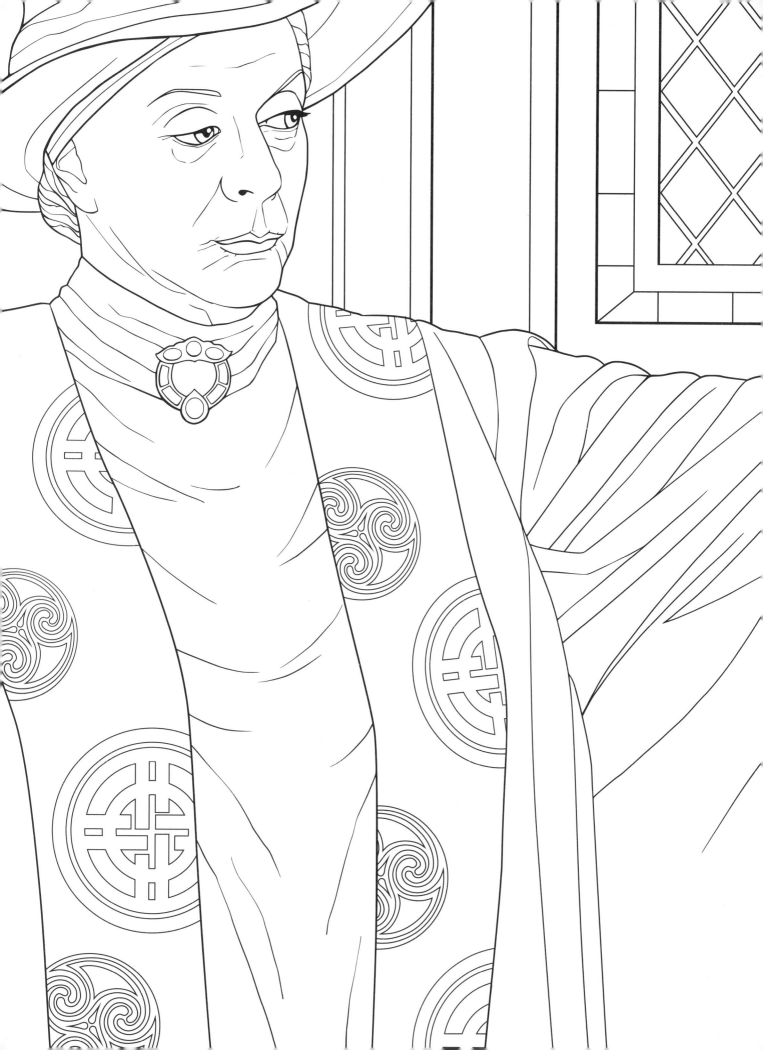

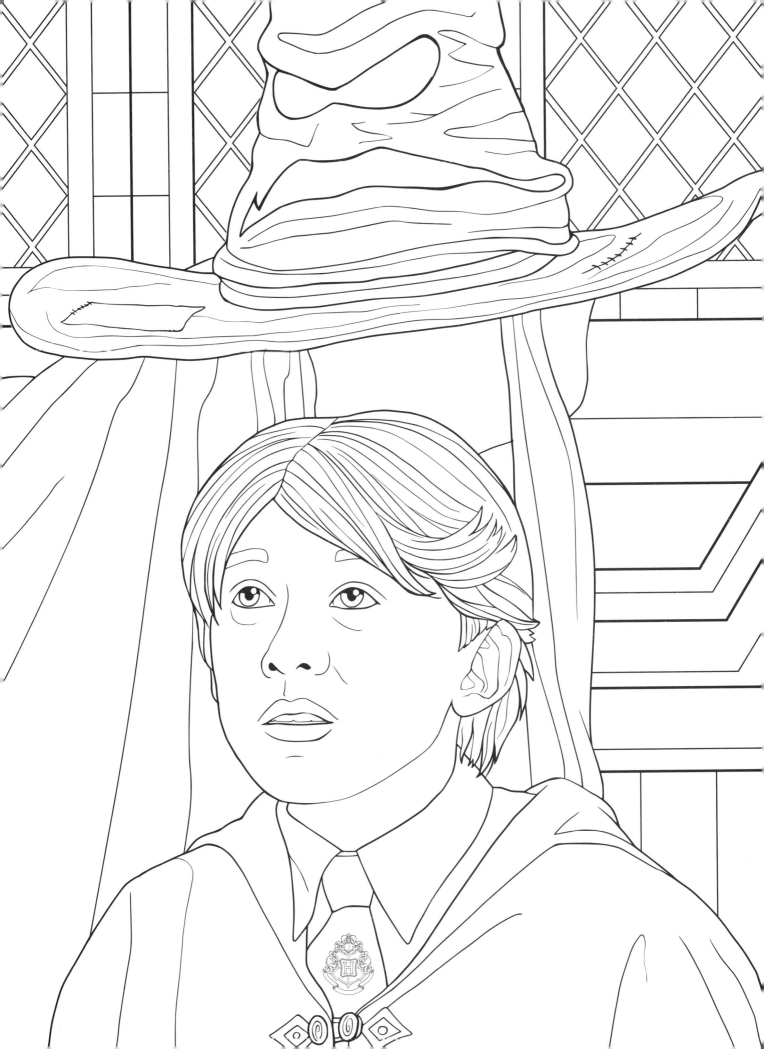

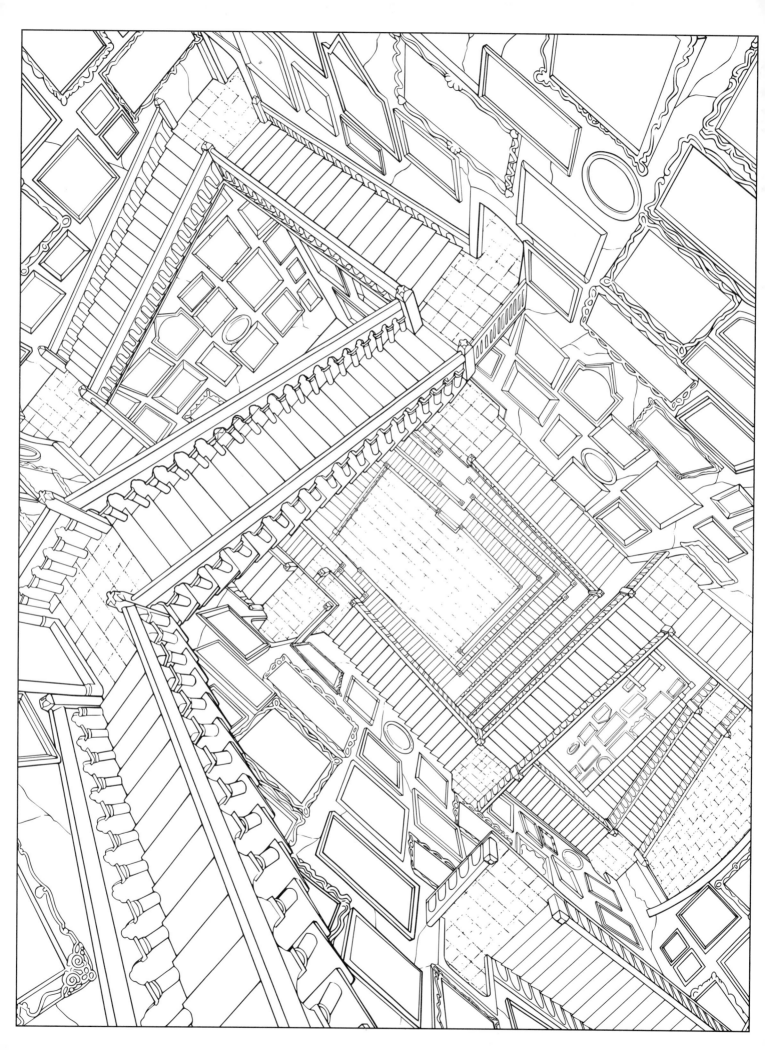

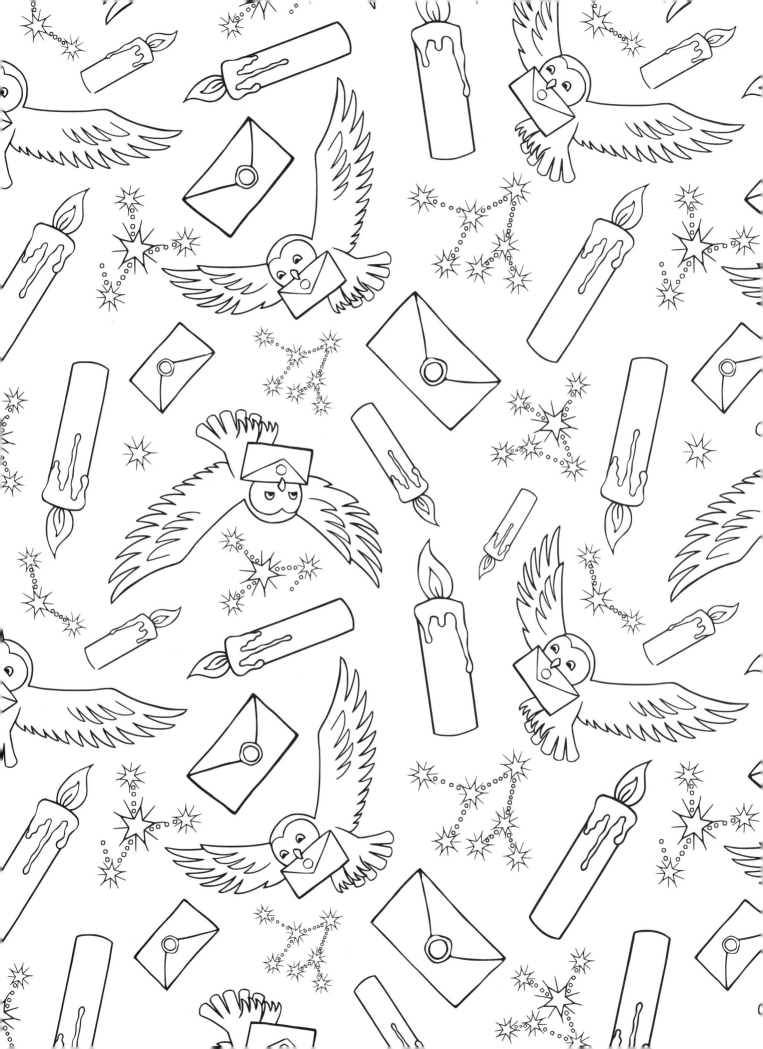

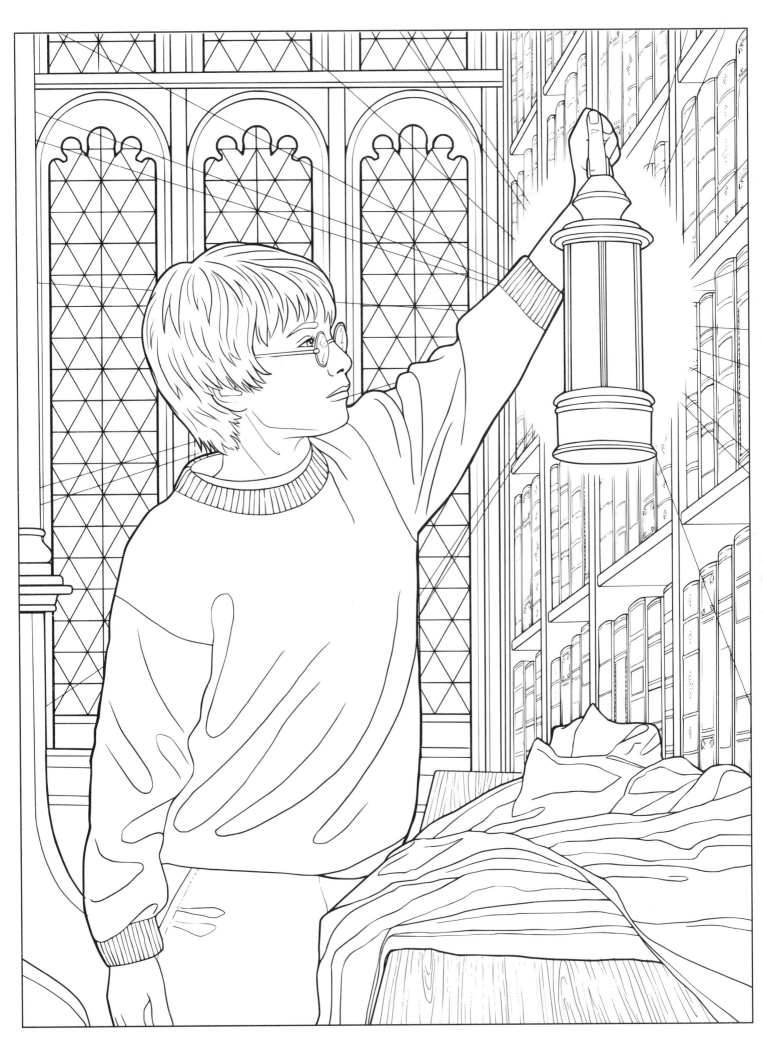

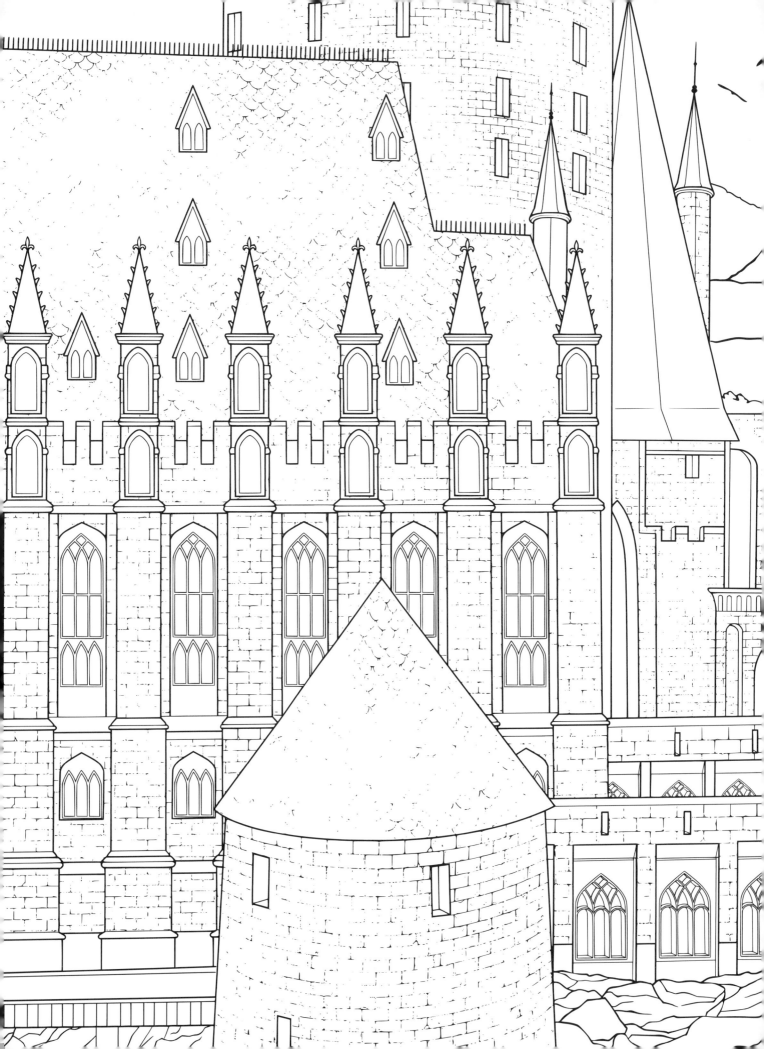

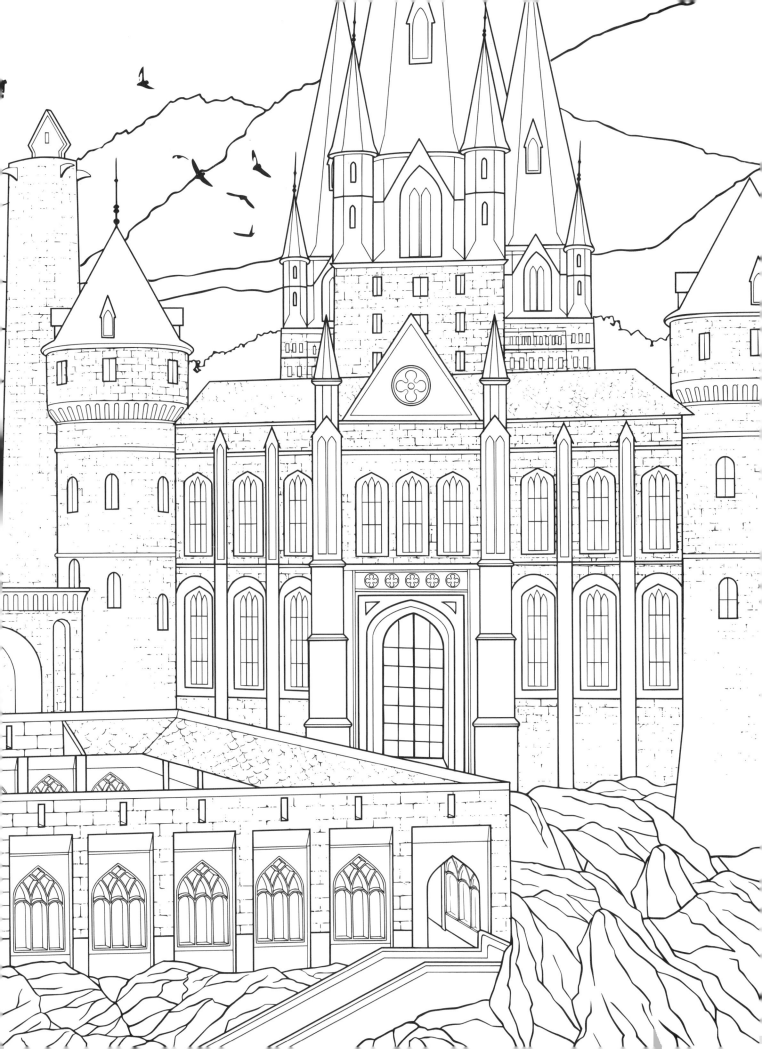

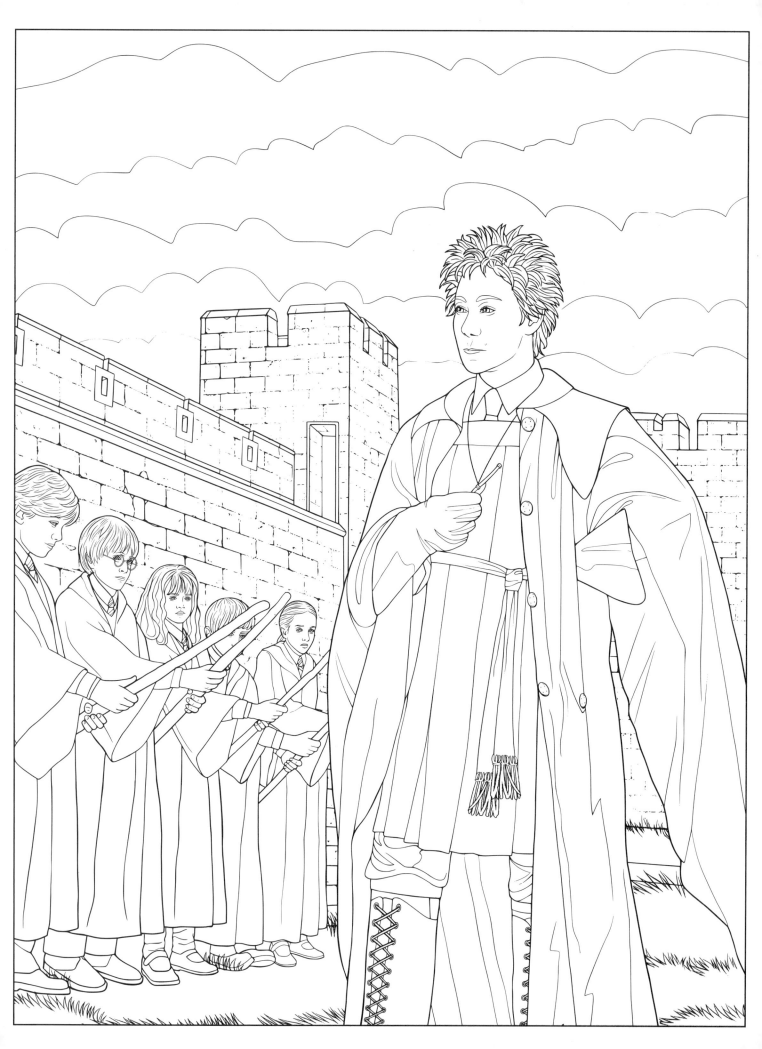

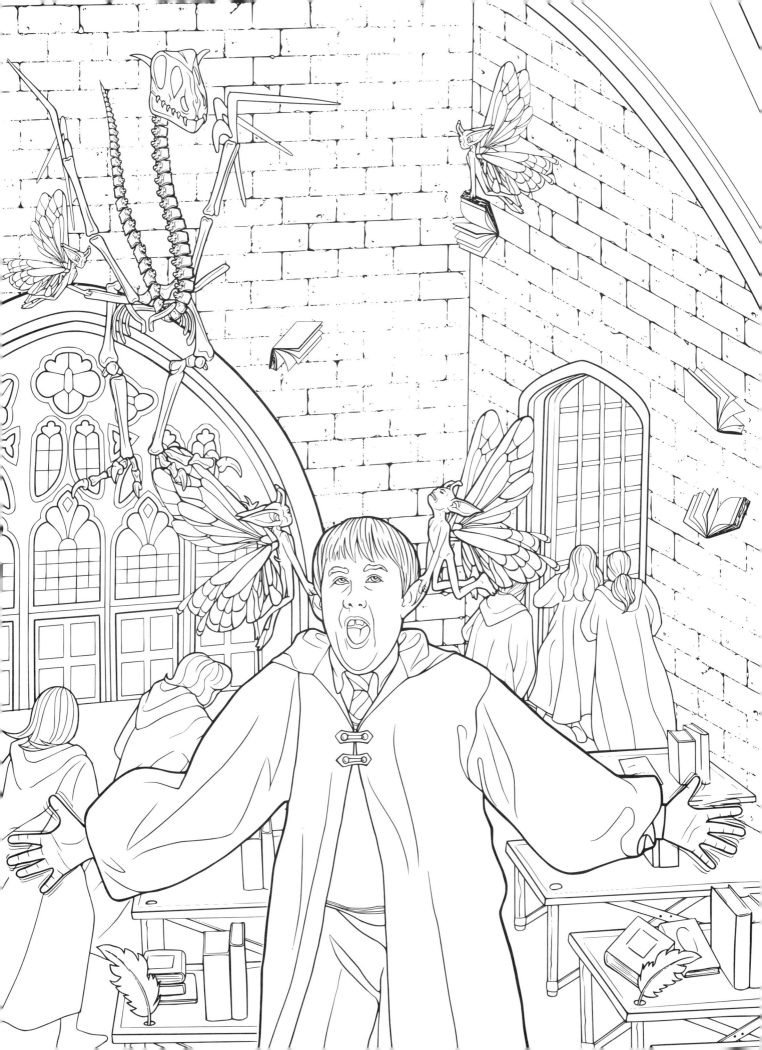

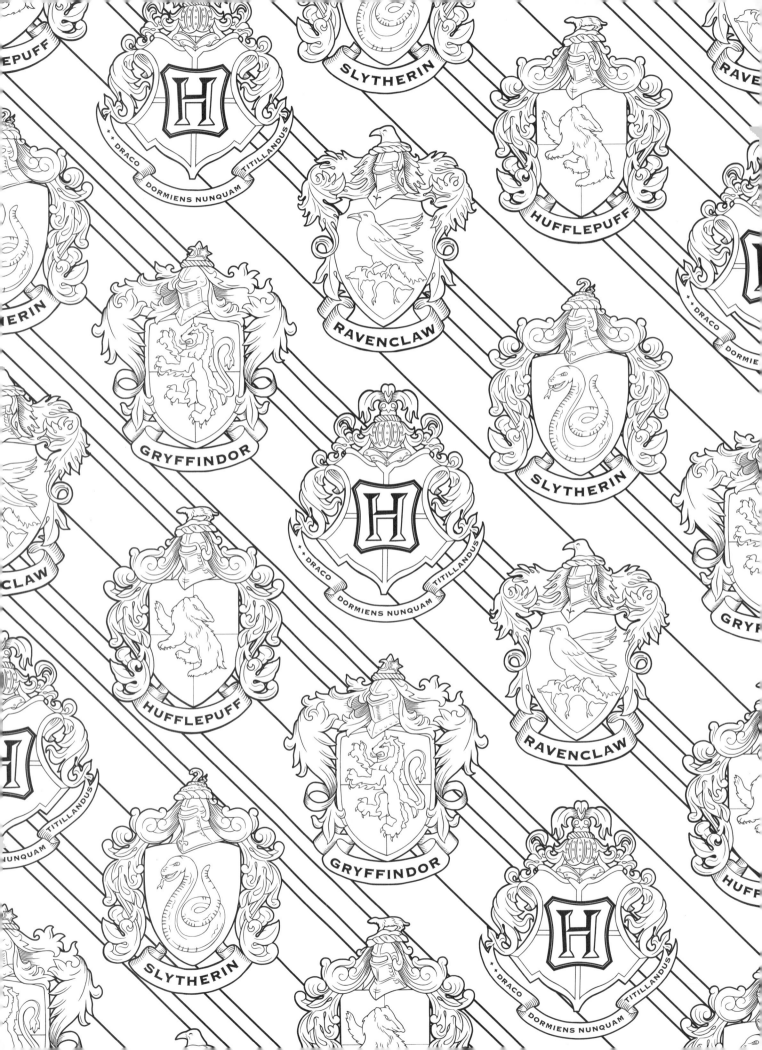

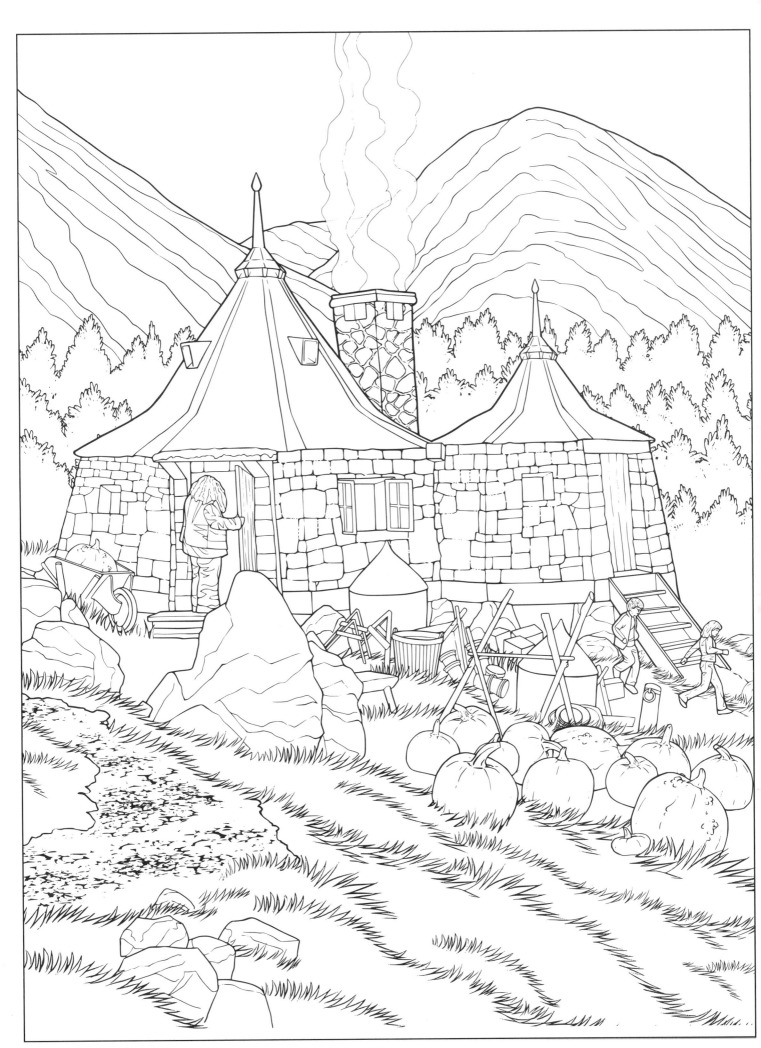

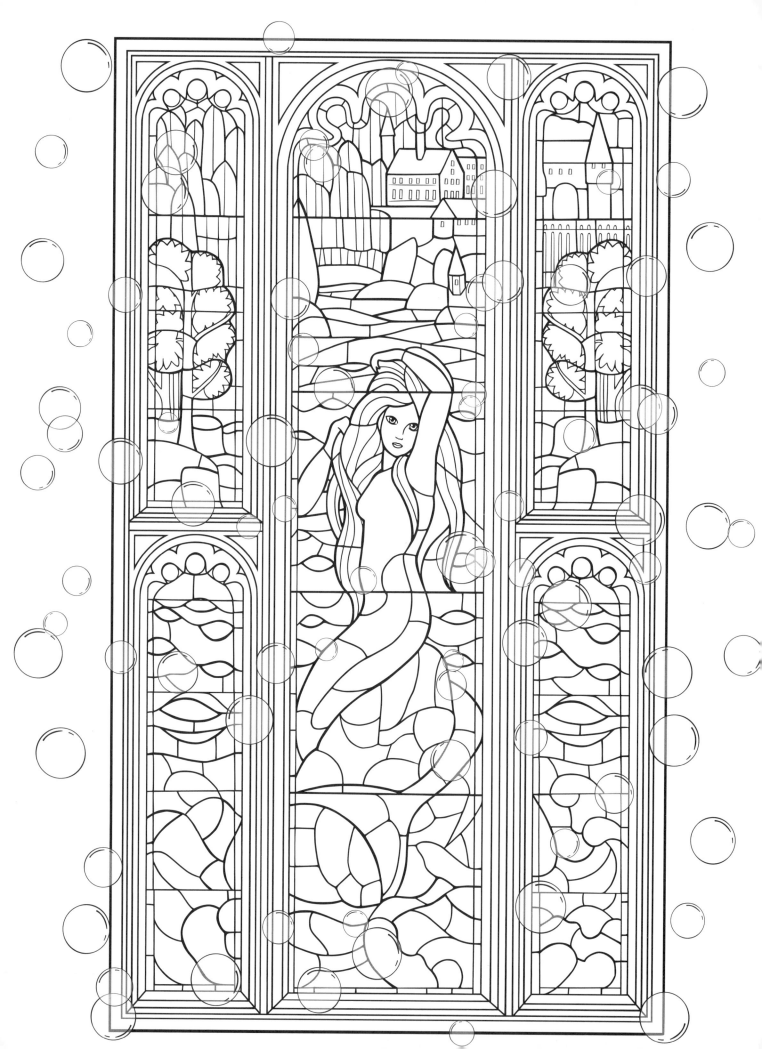

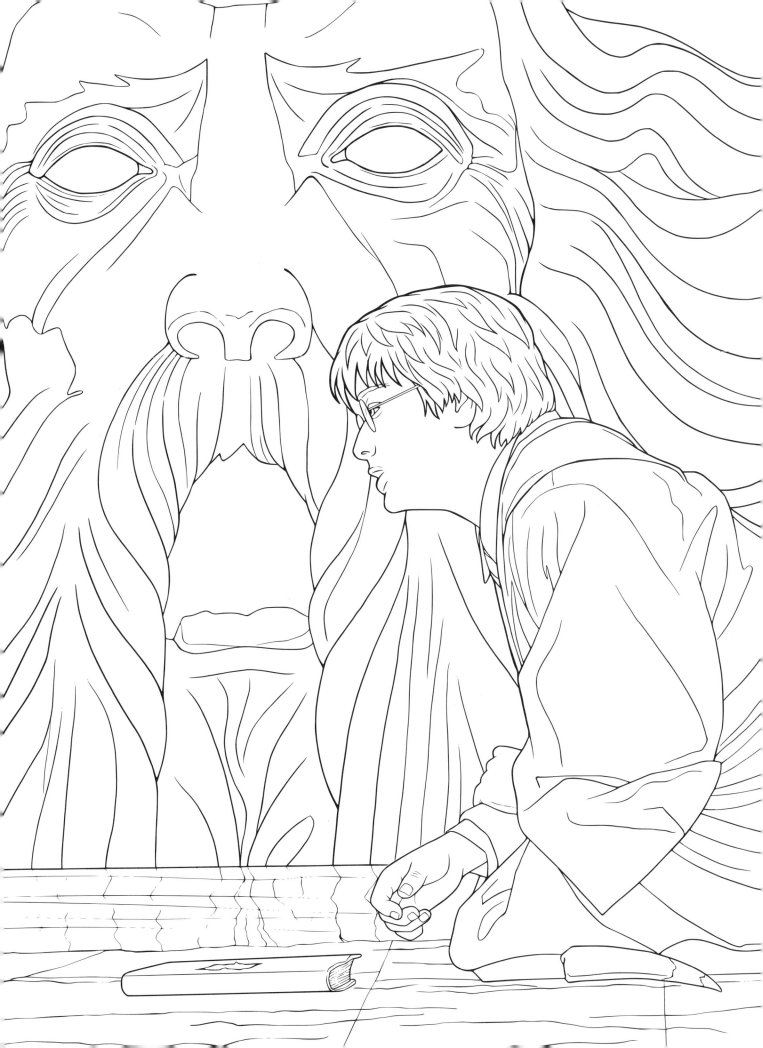

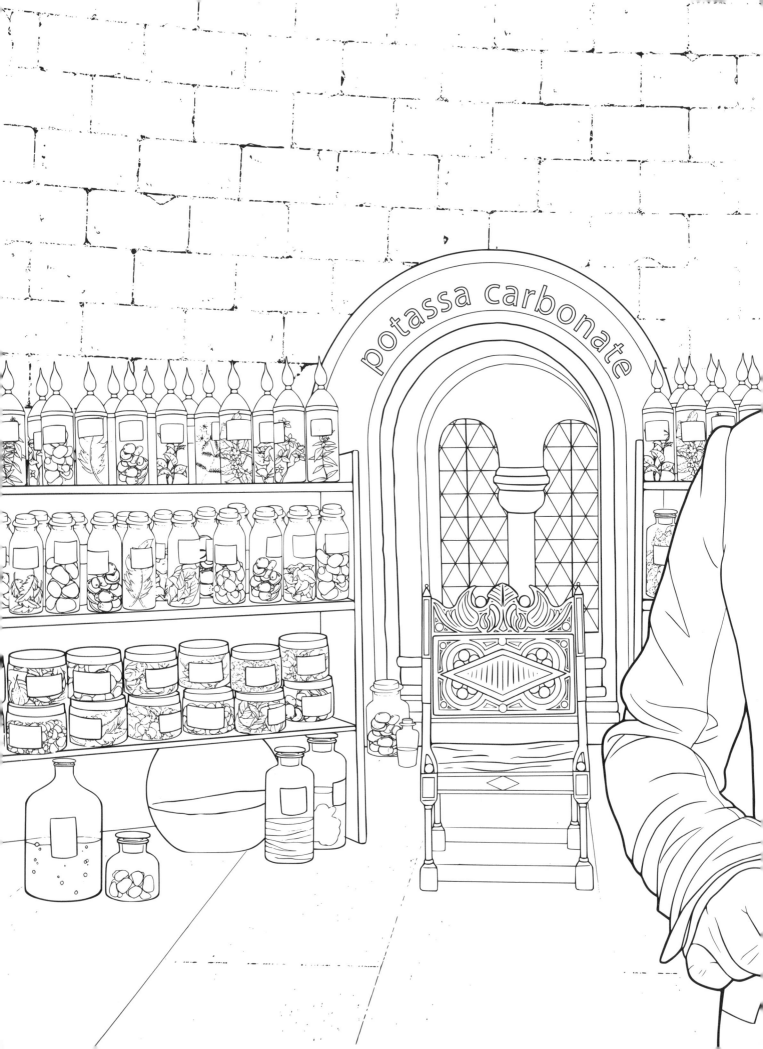

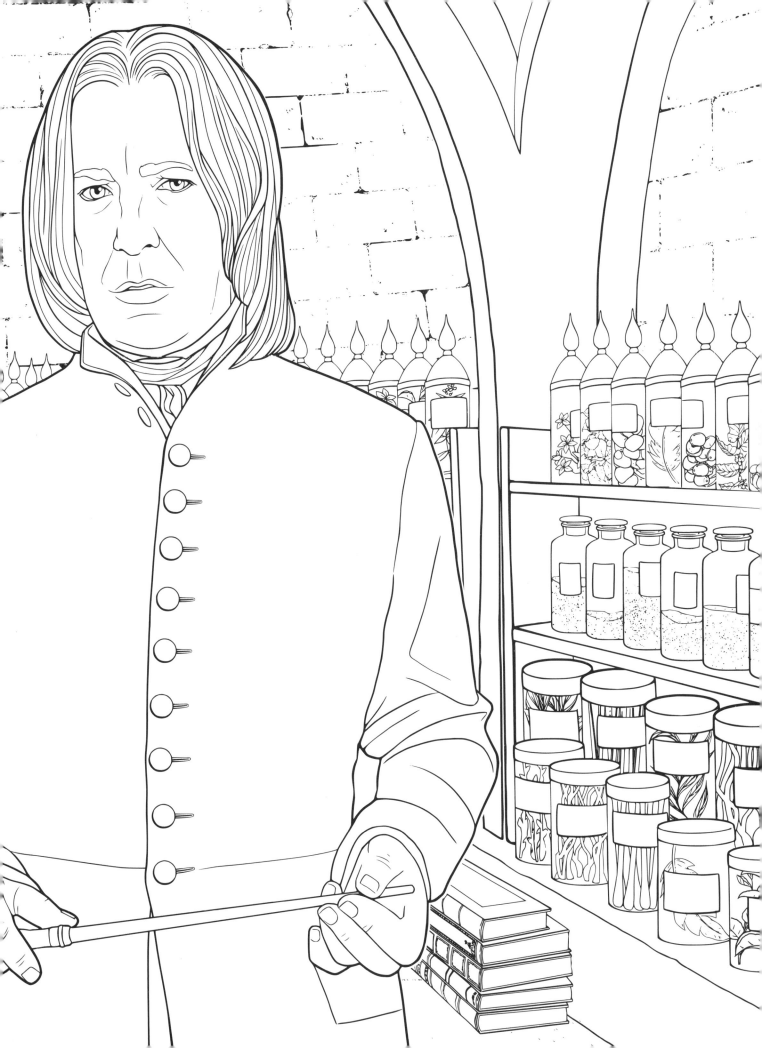

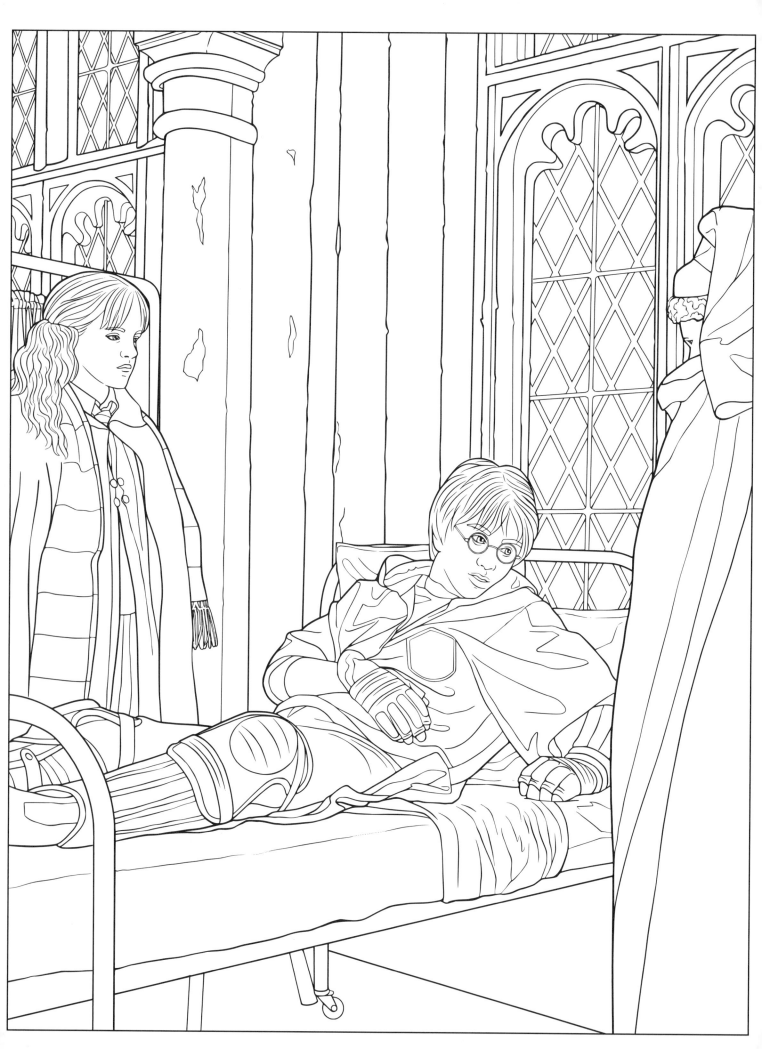

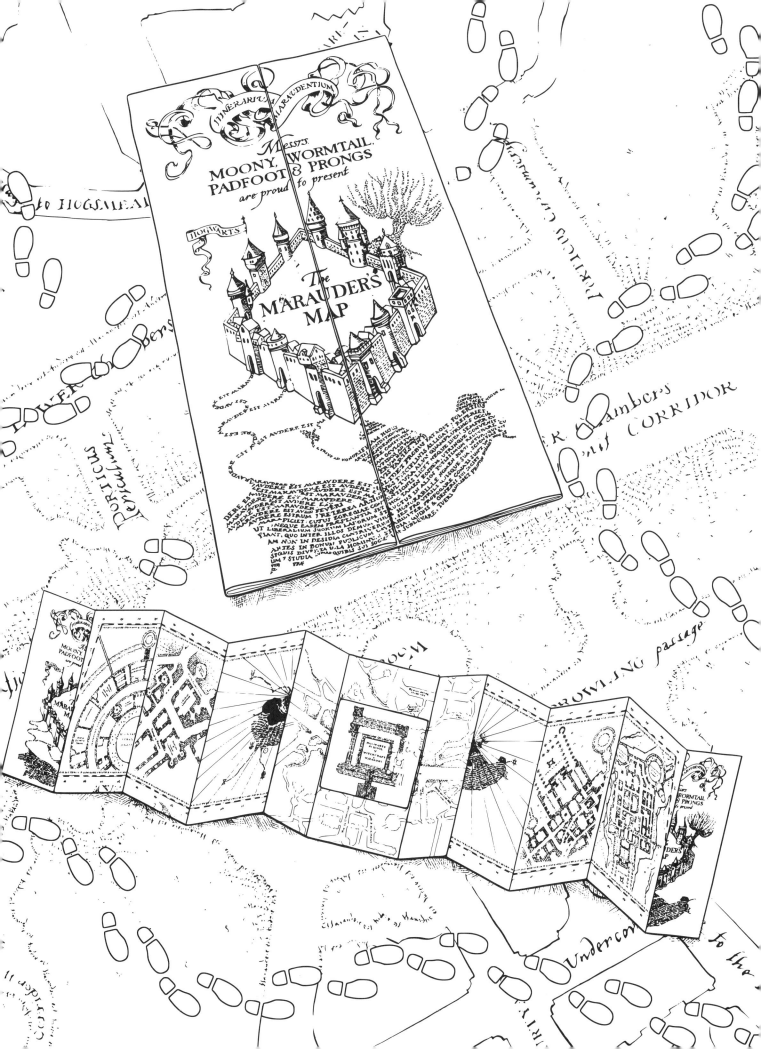

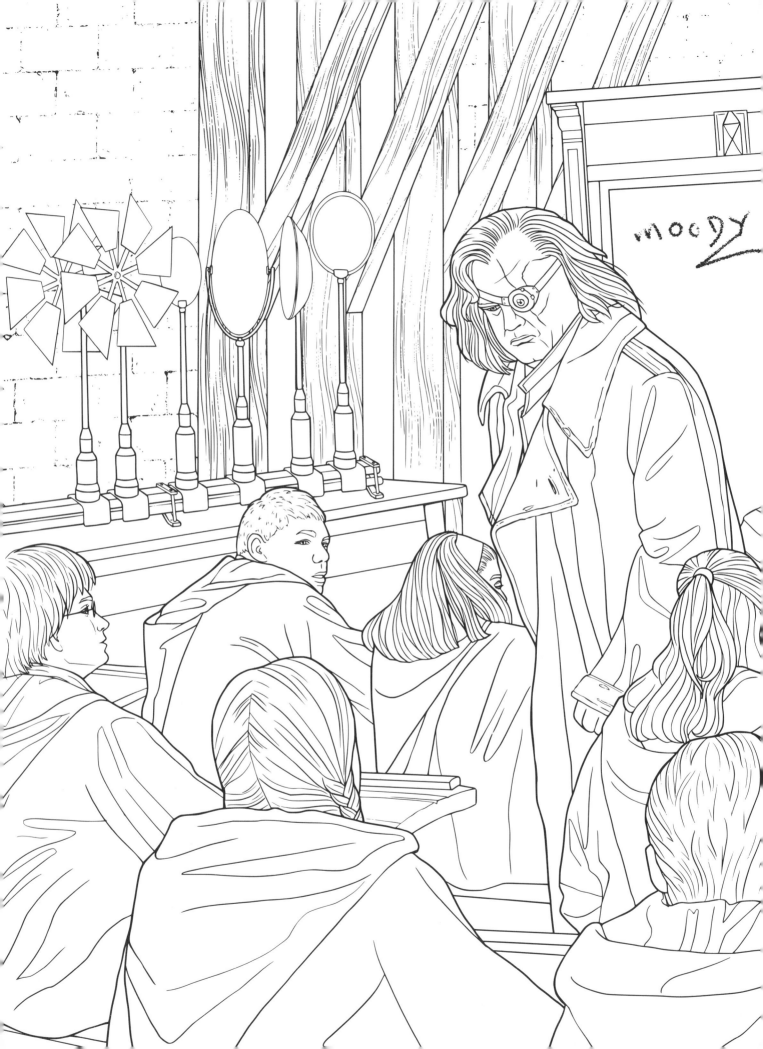

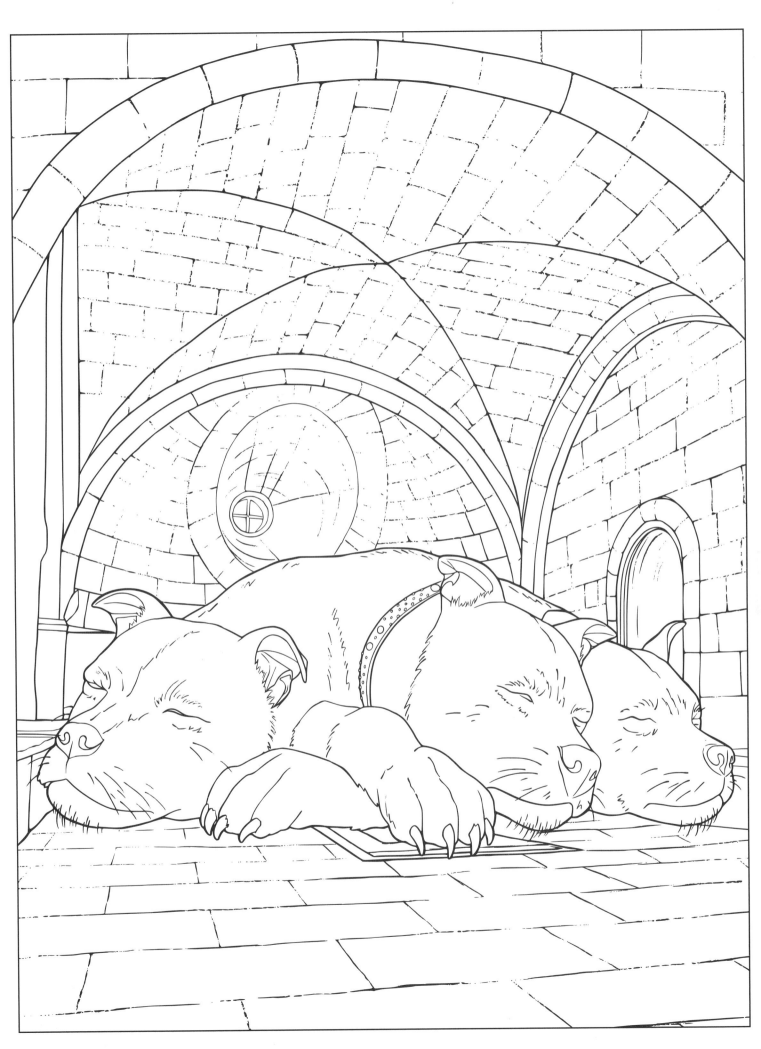

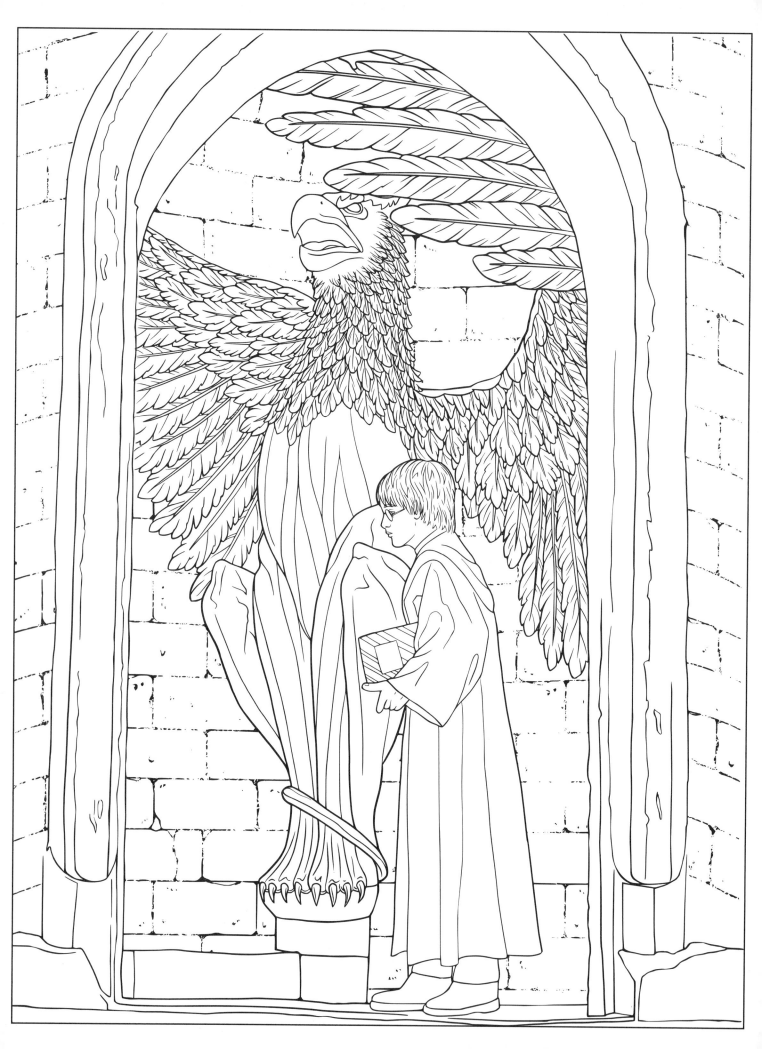

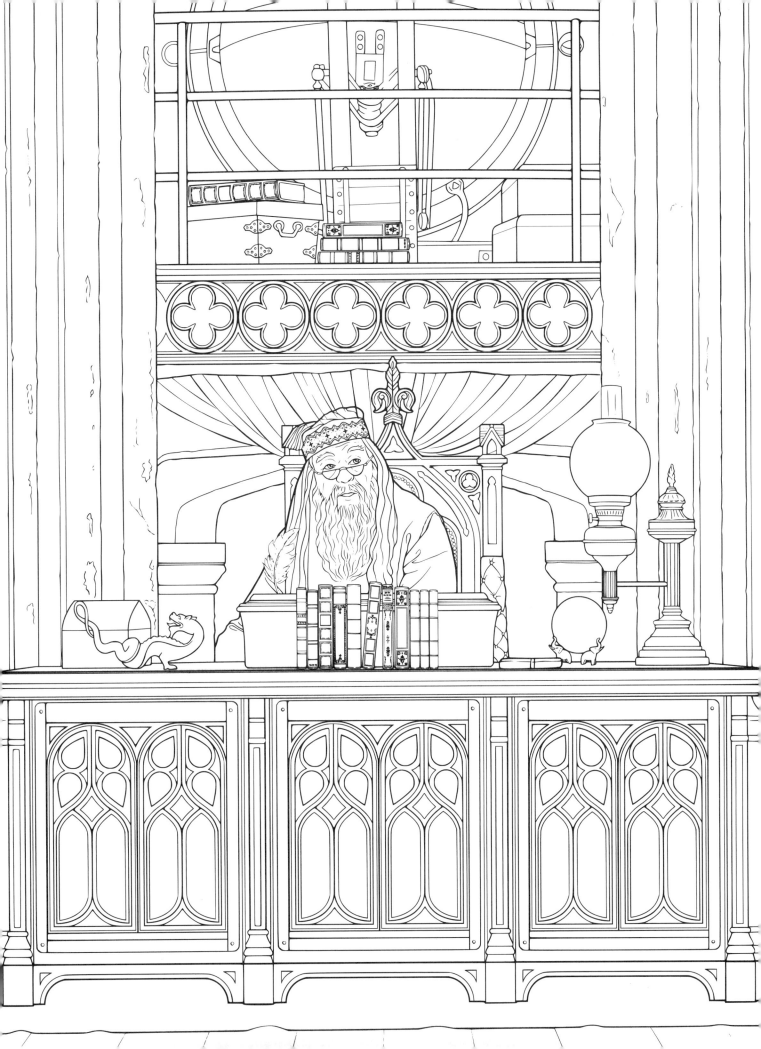

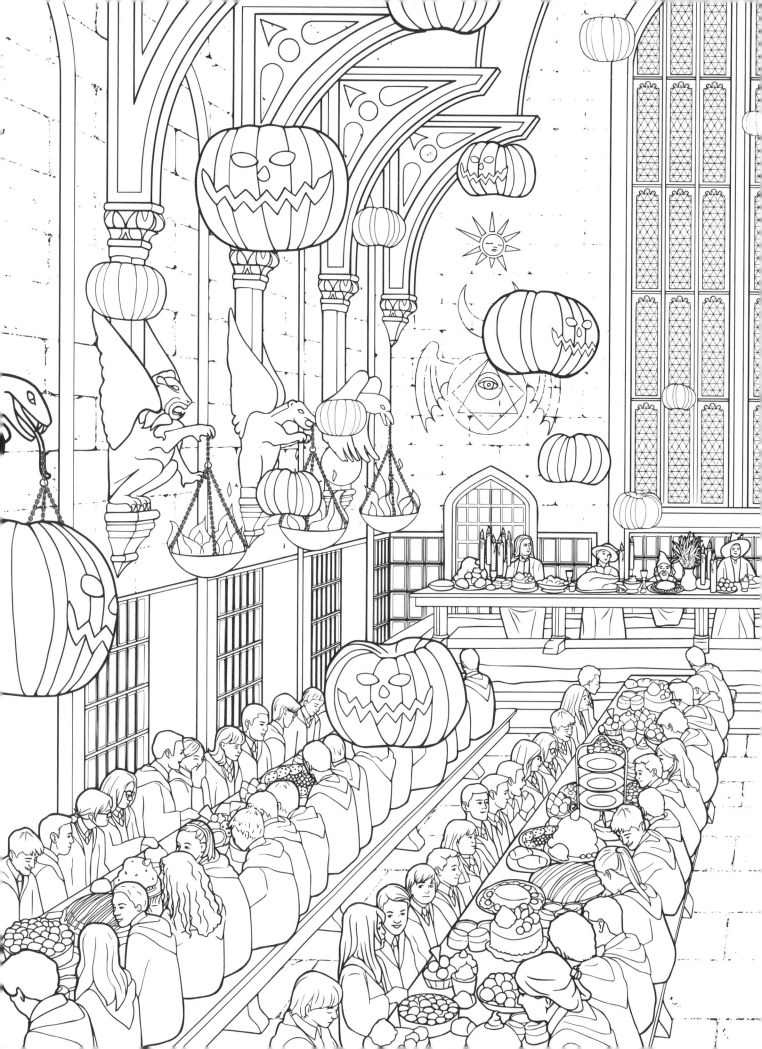

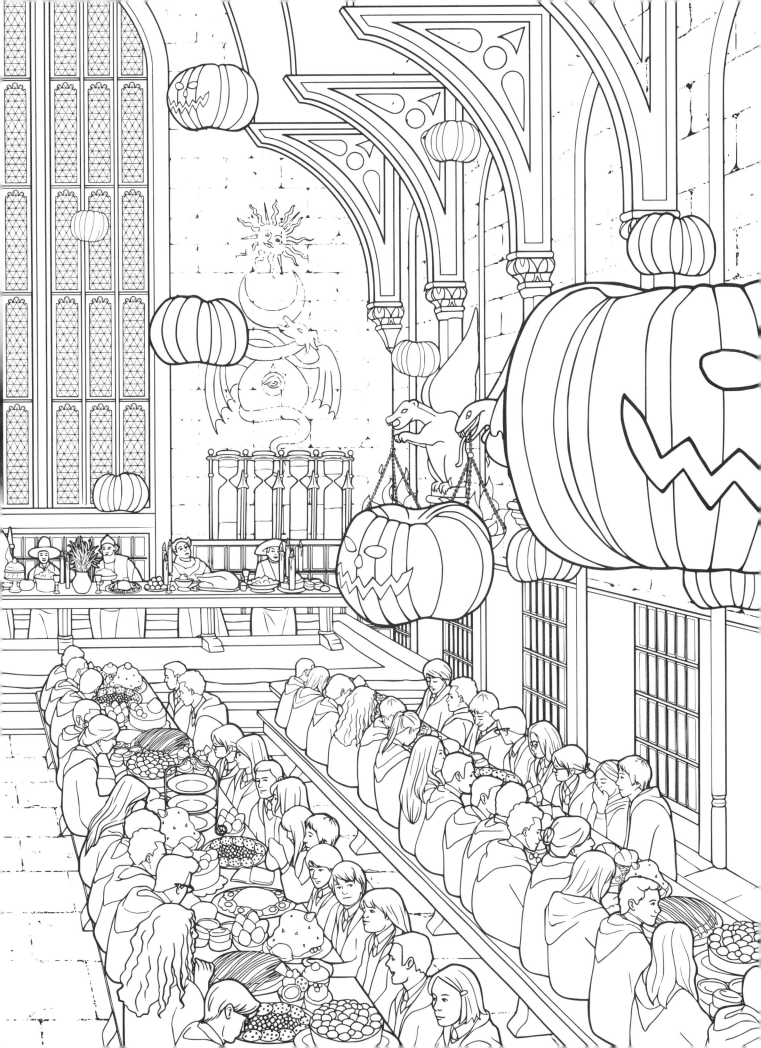

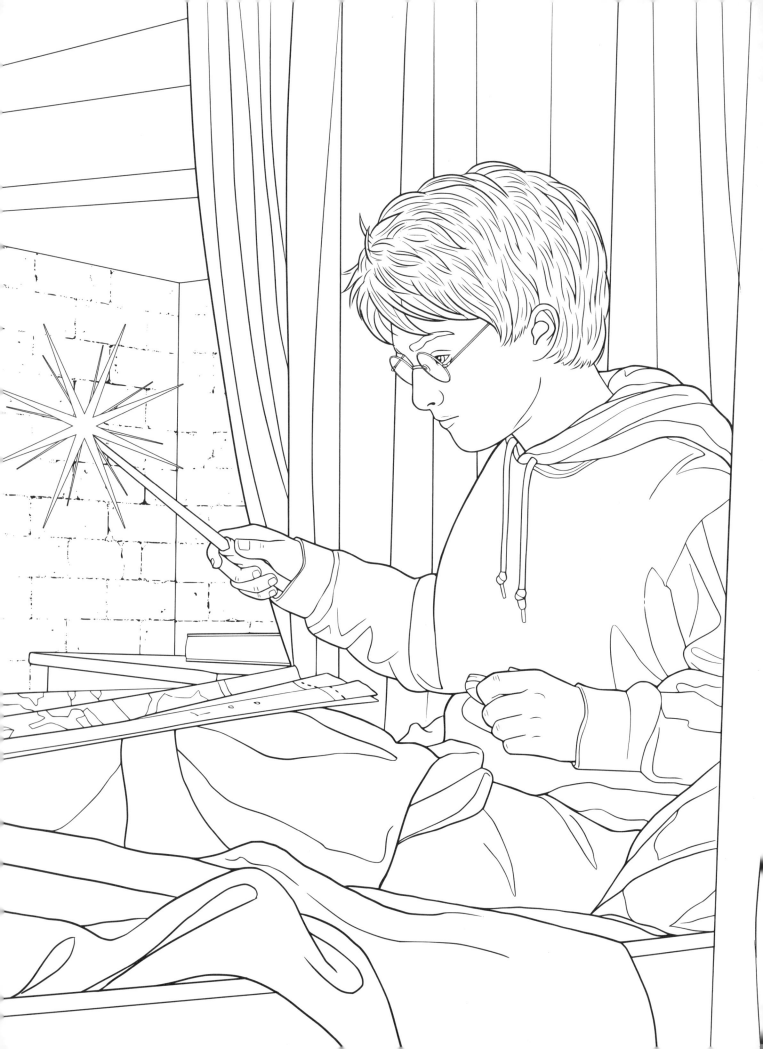

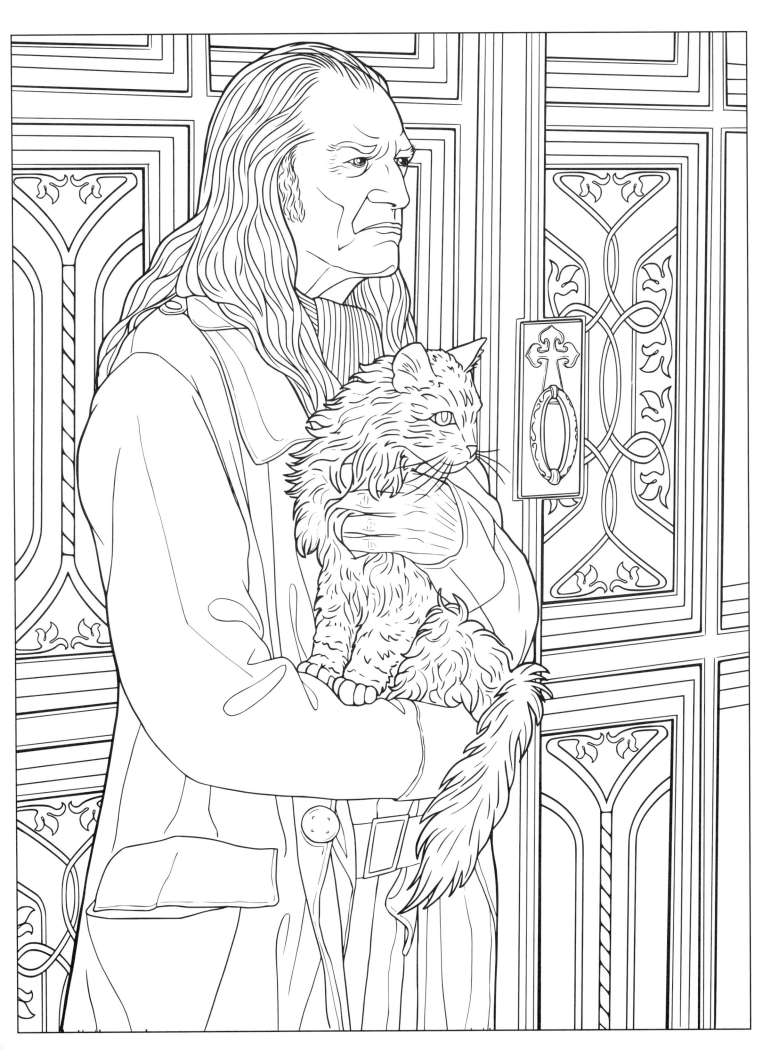

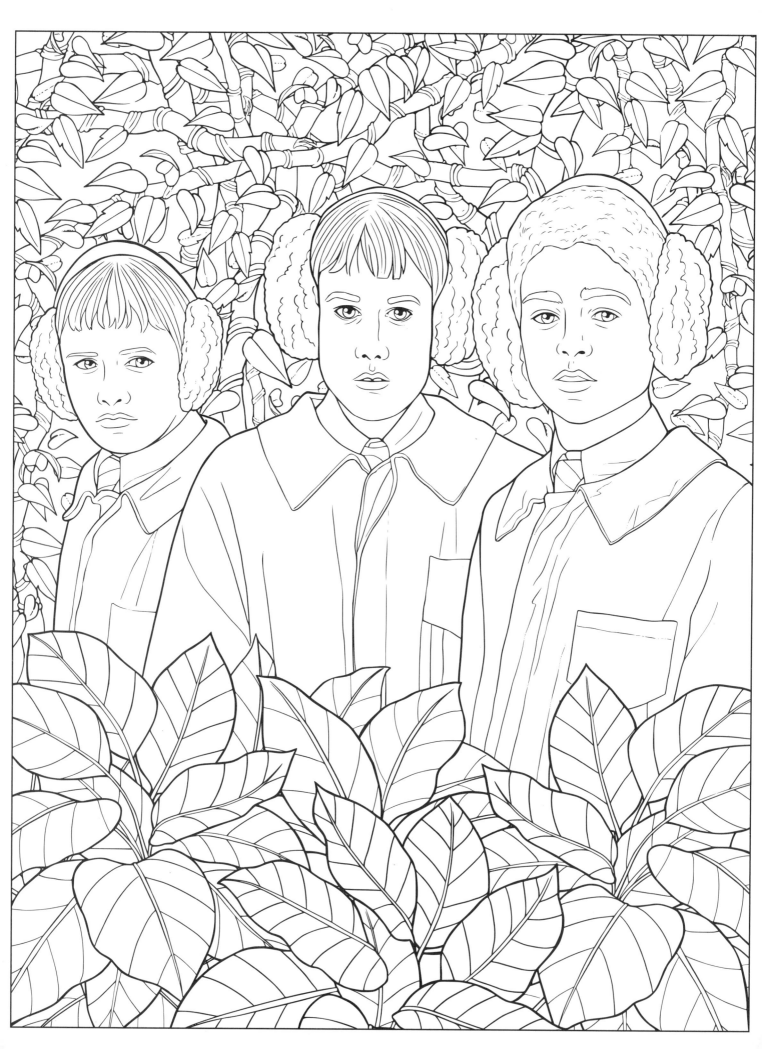

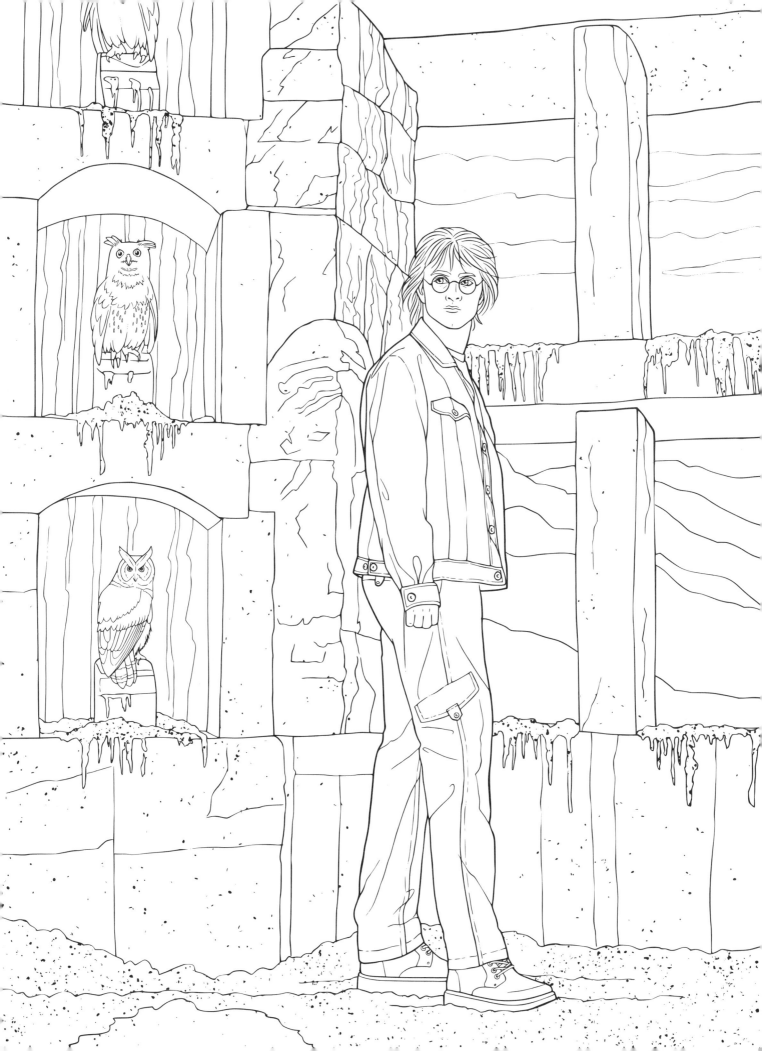

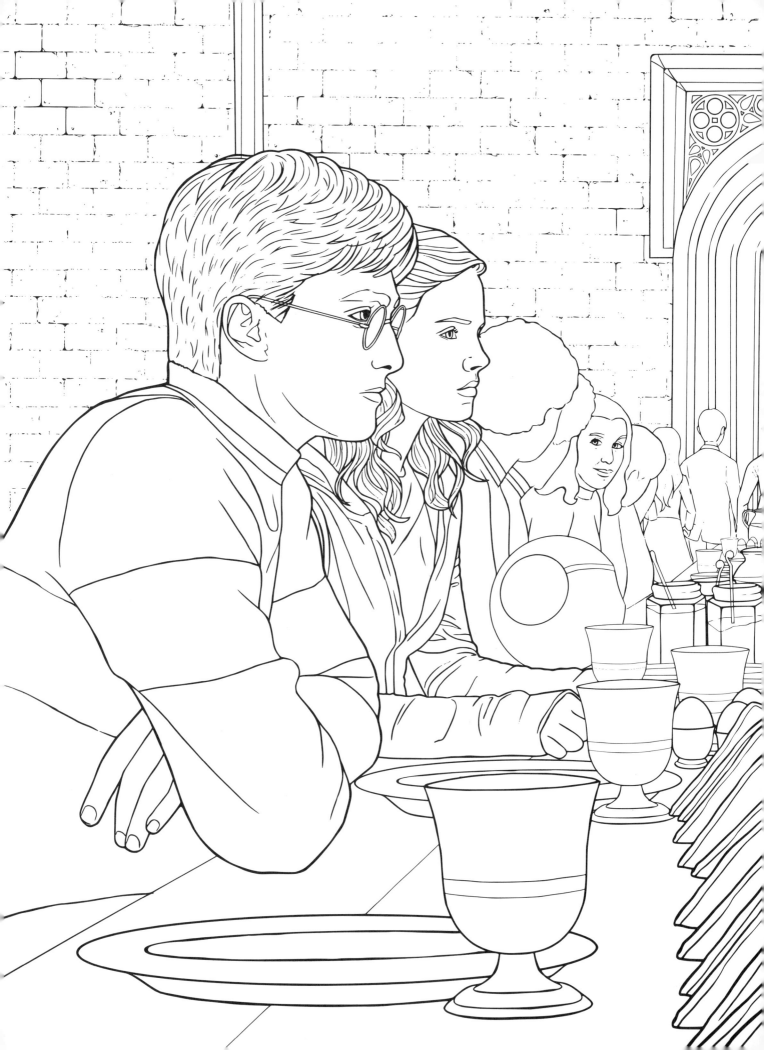

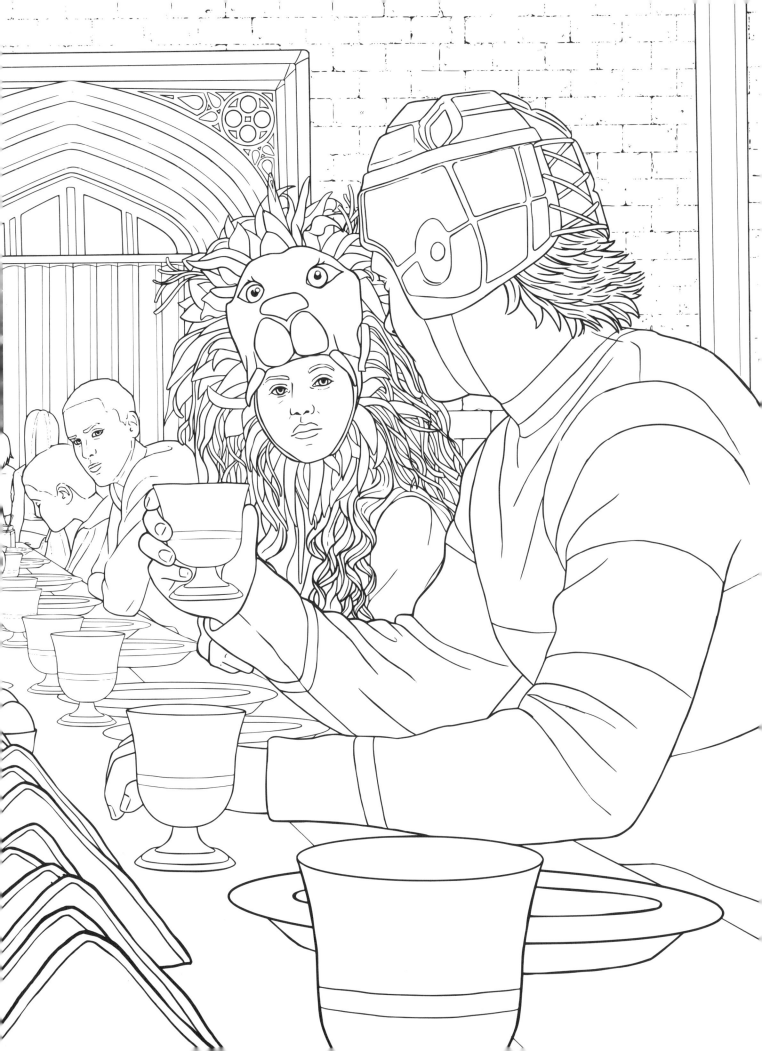

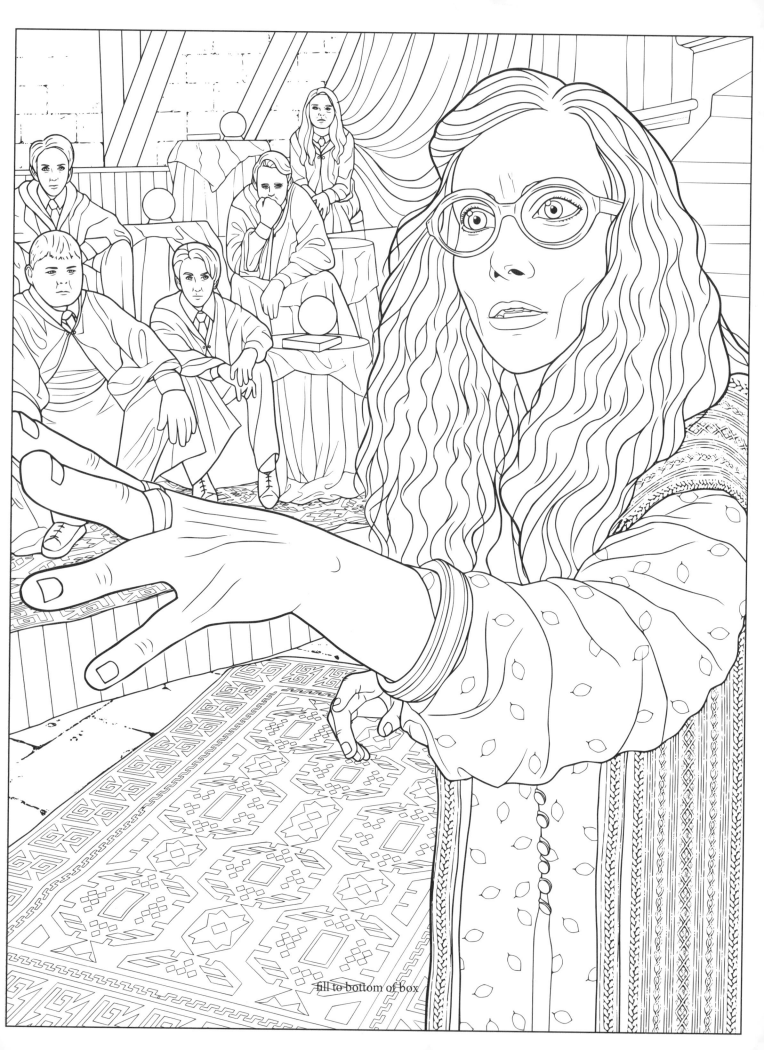

fill to bottom of box

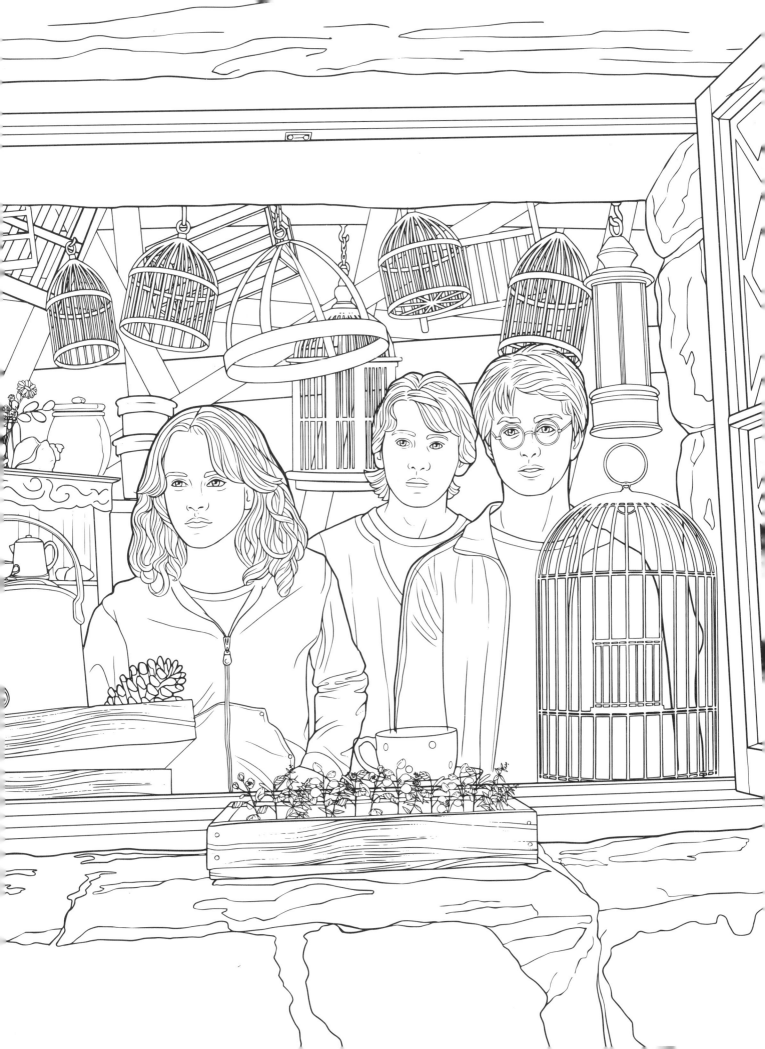

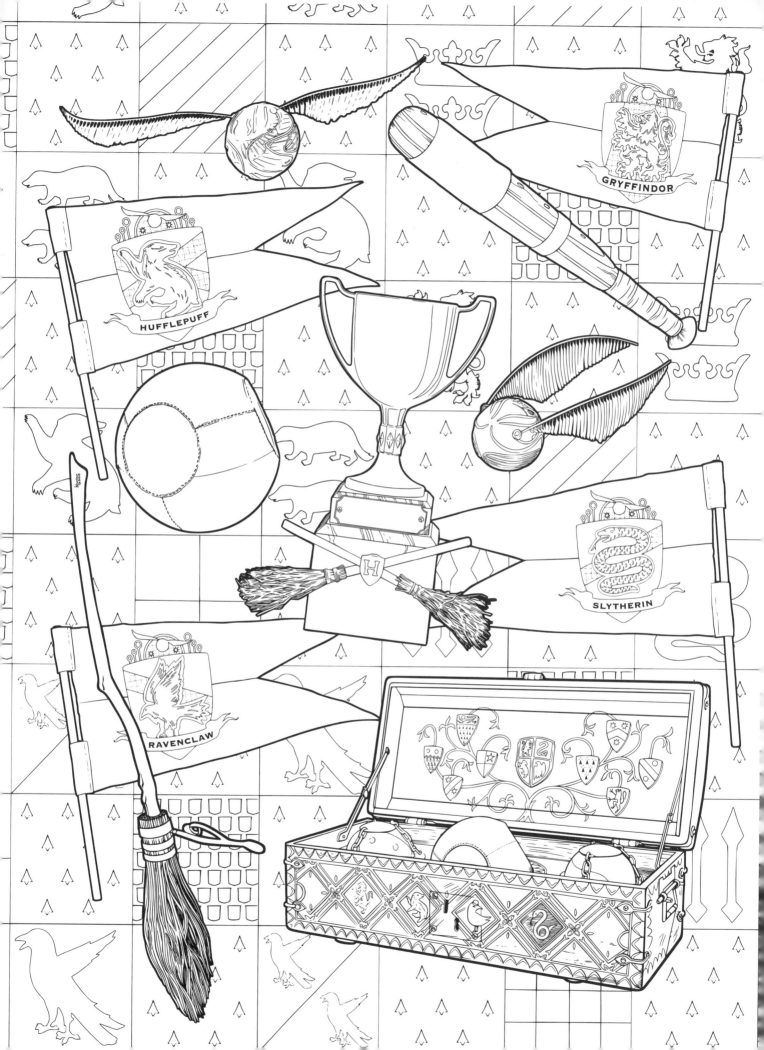

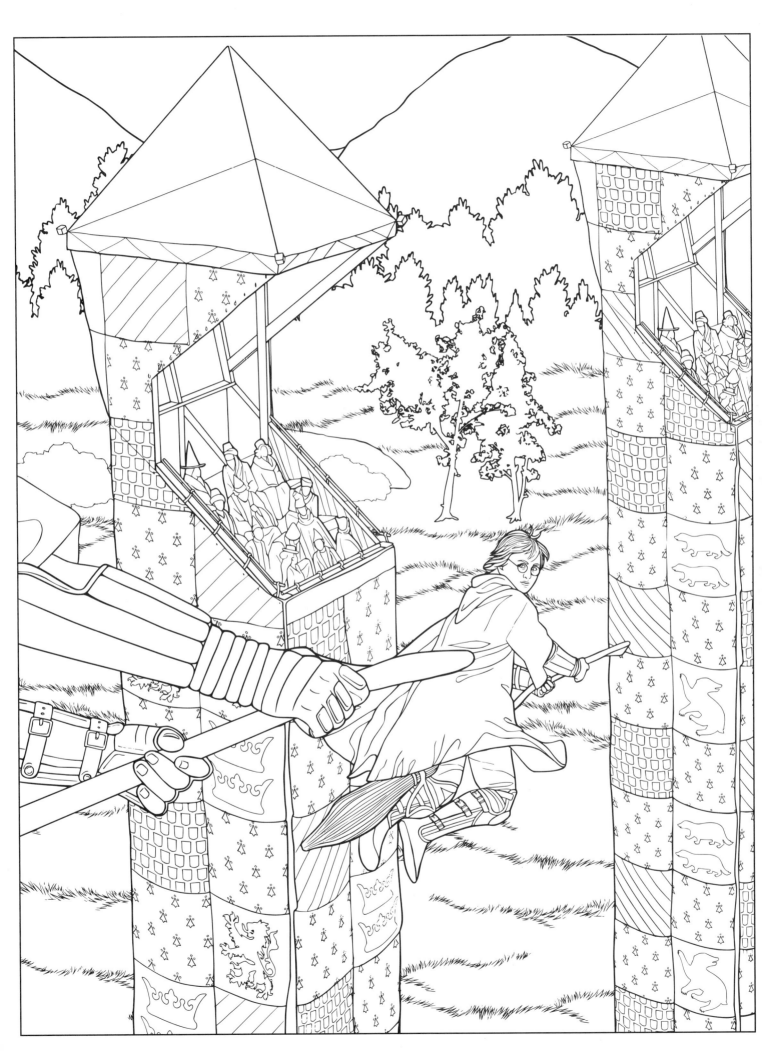

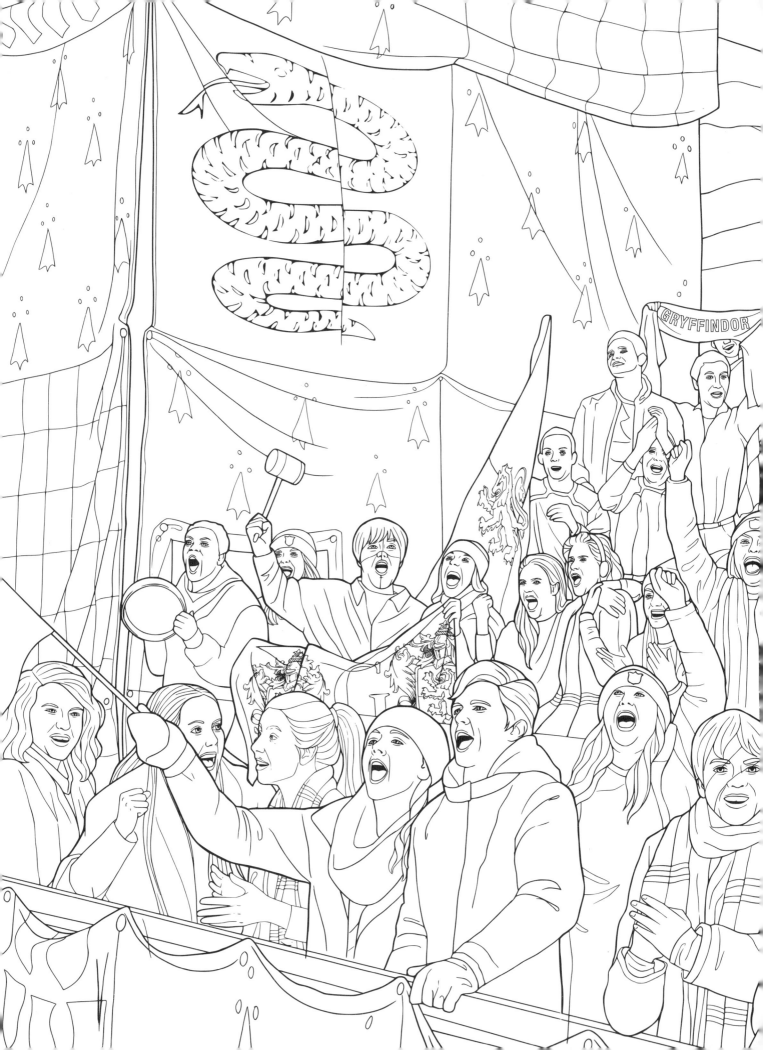

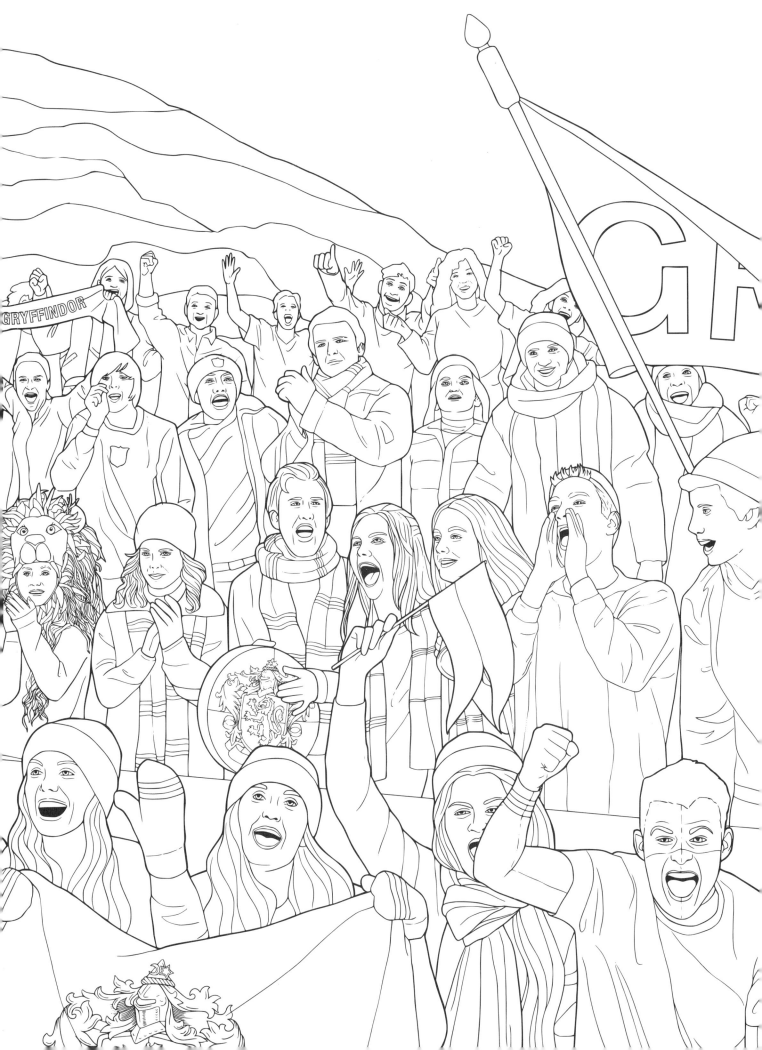

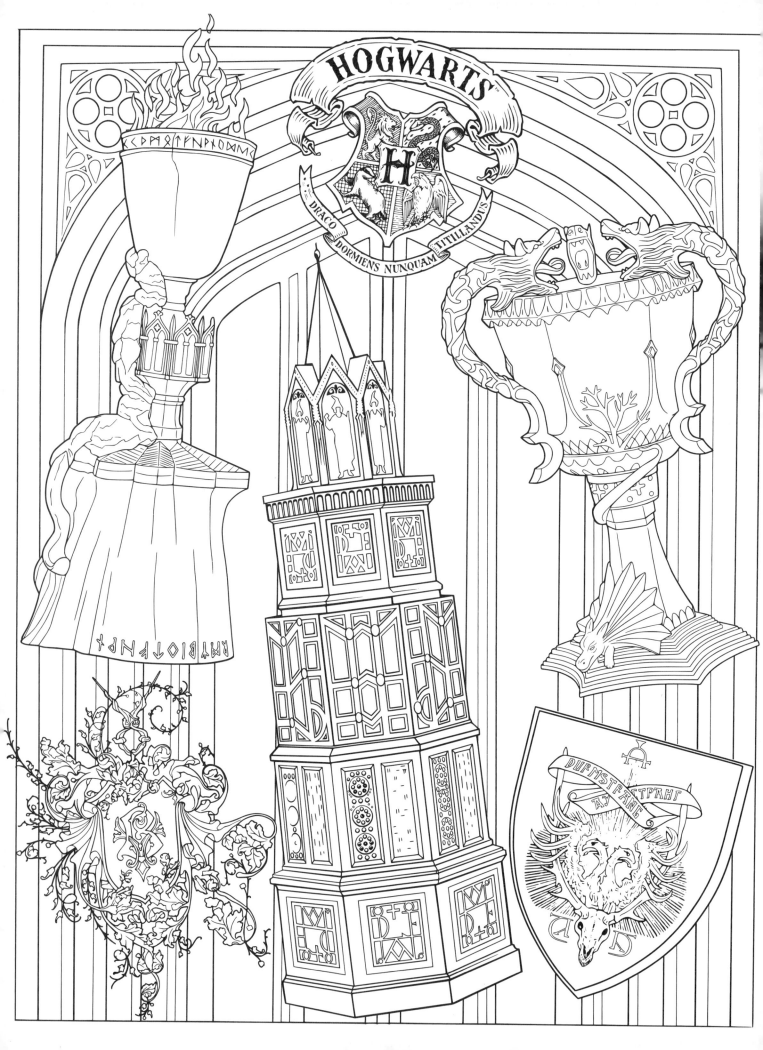

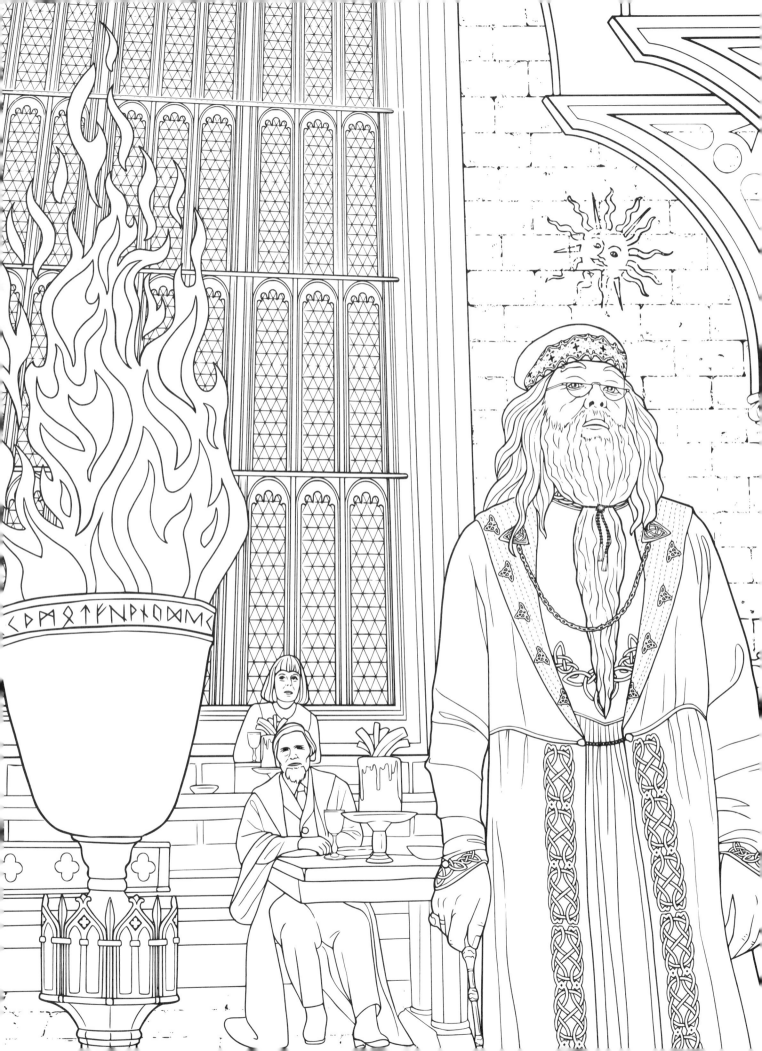

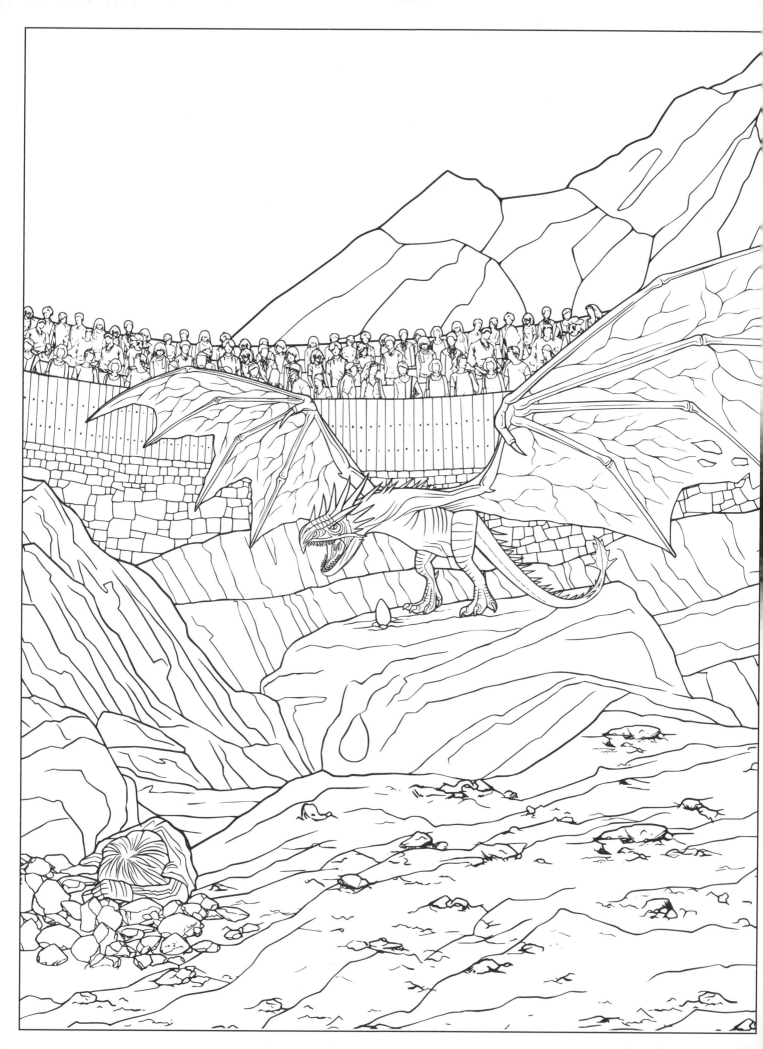

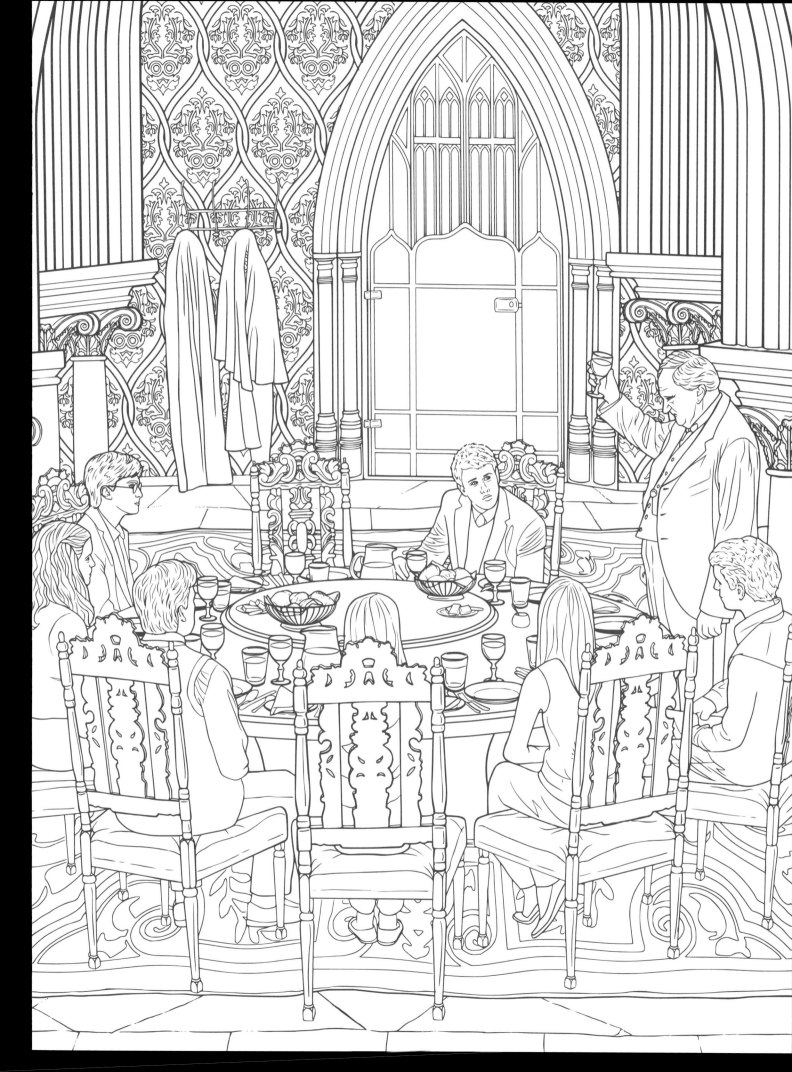

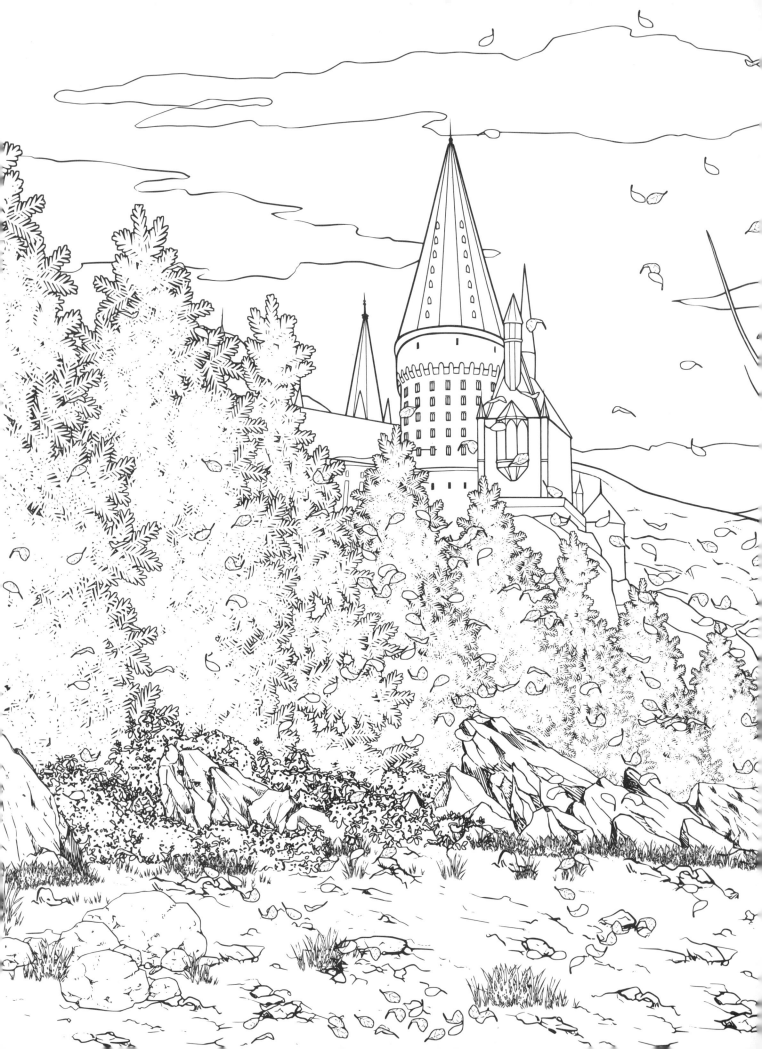

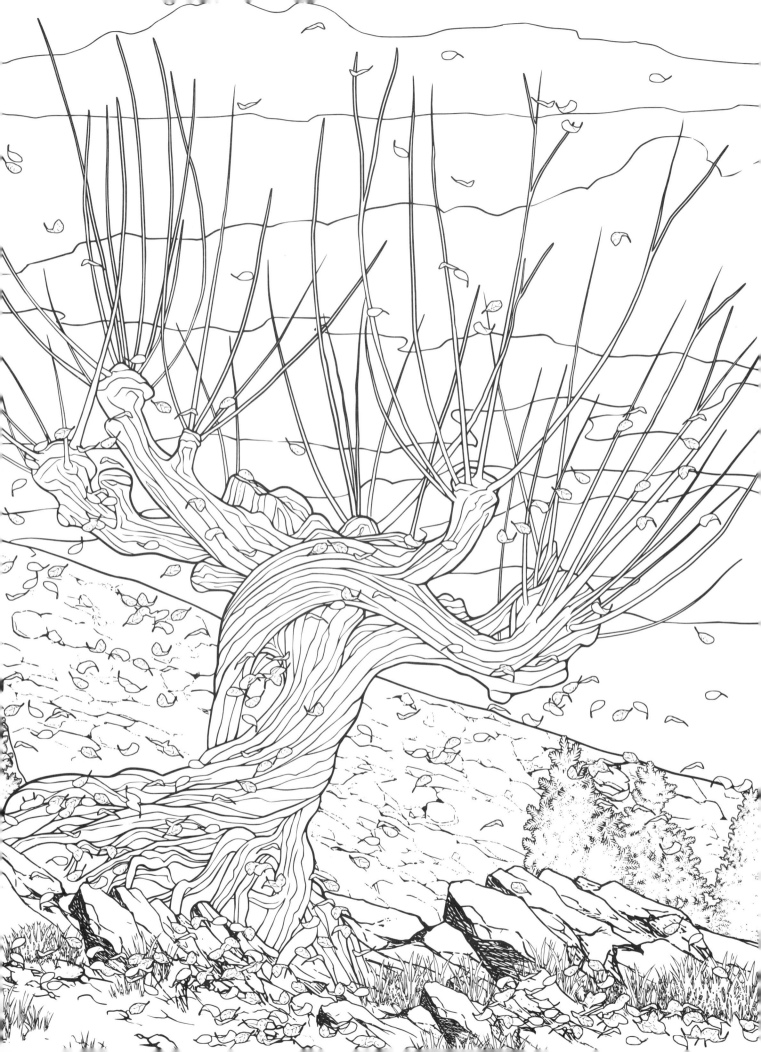

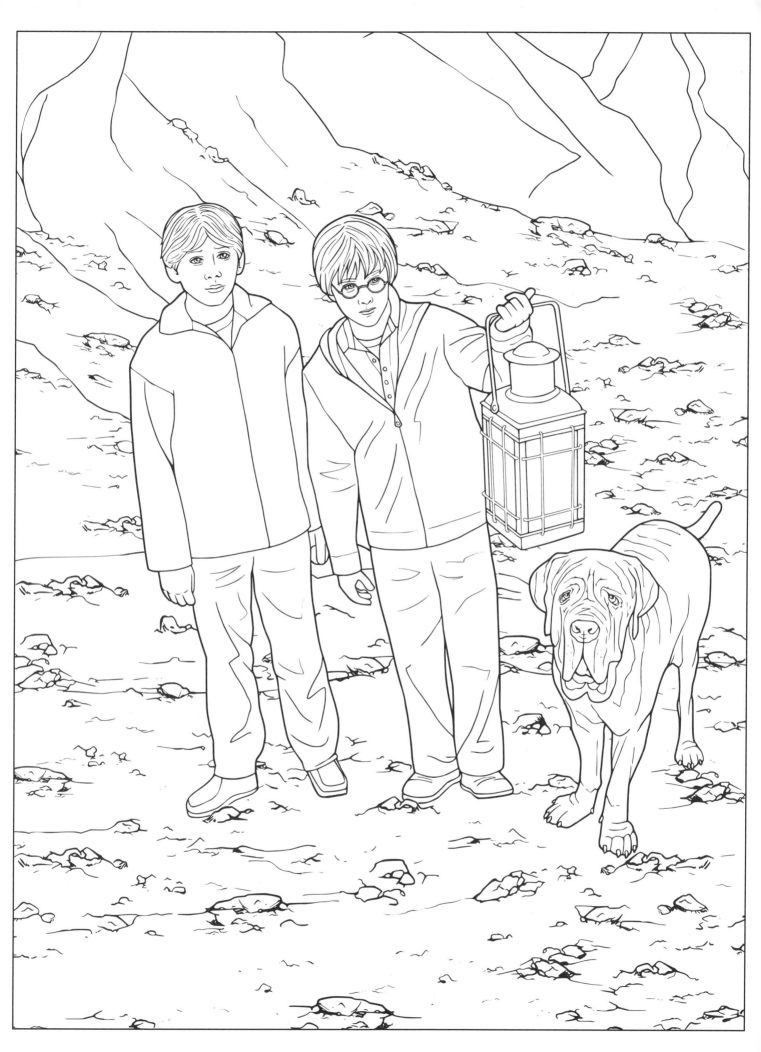

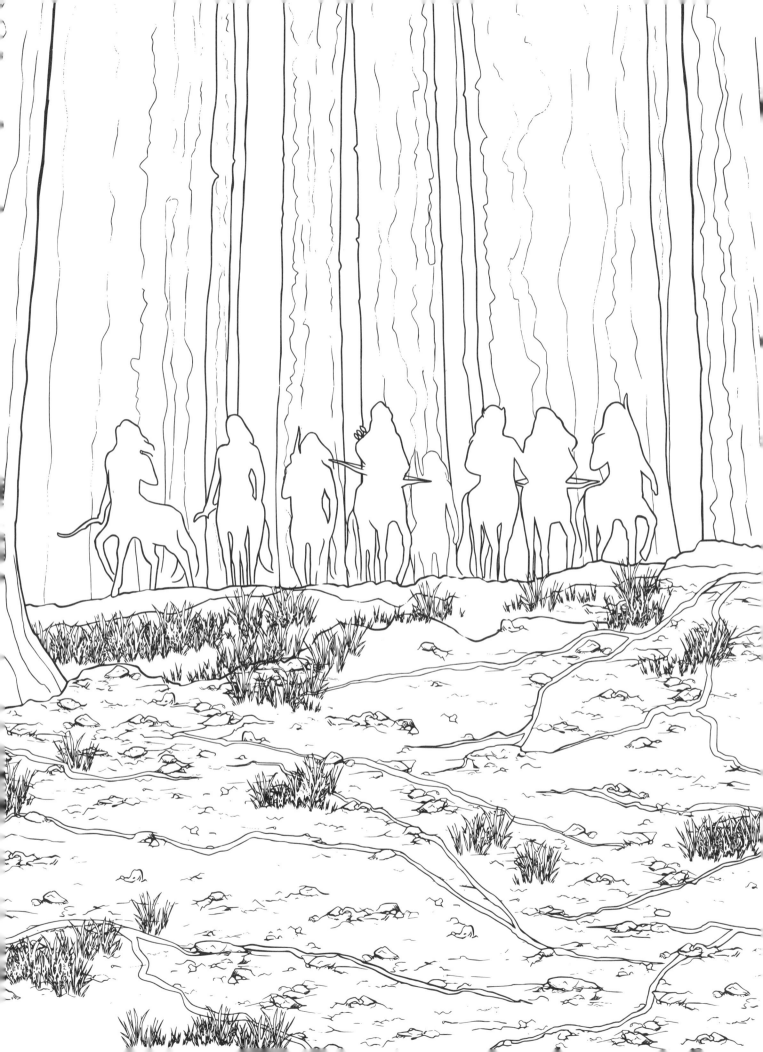

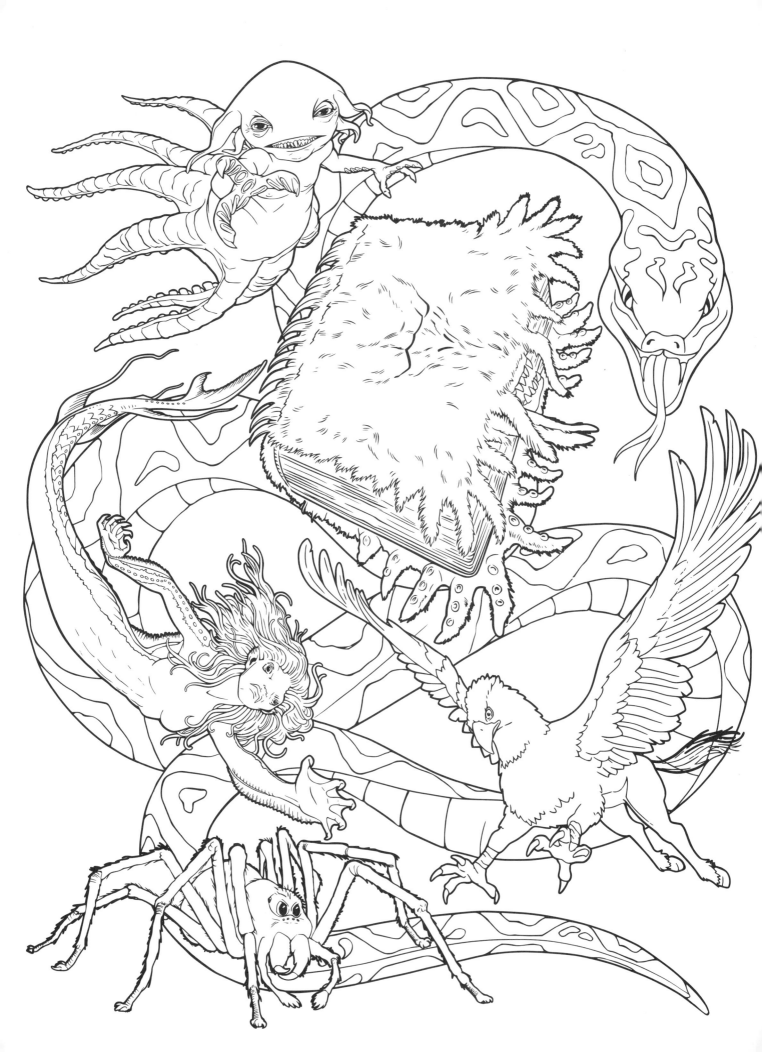

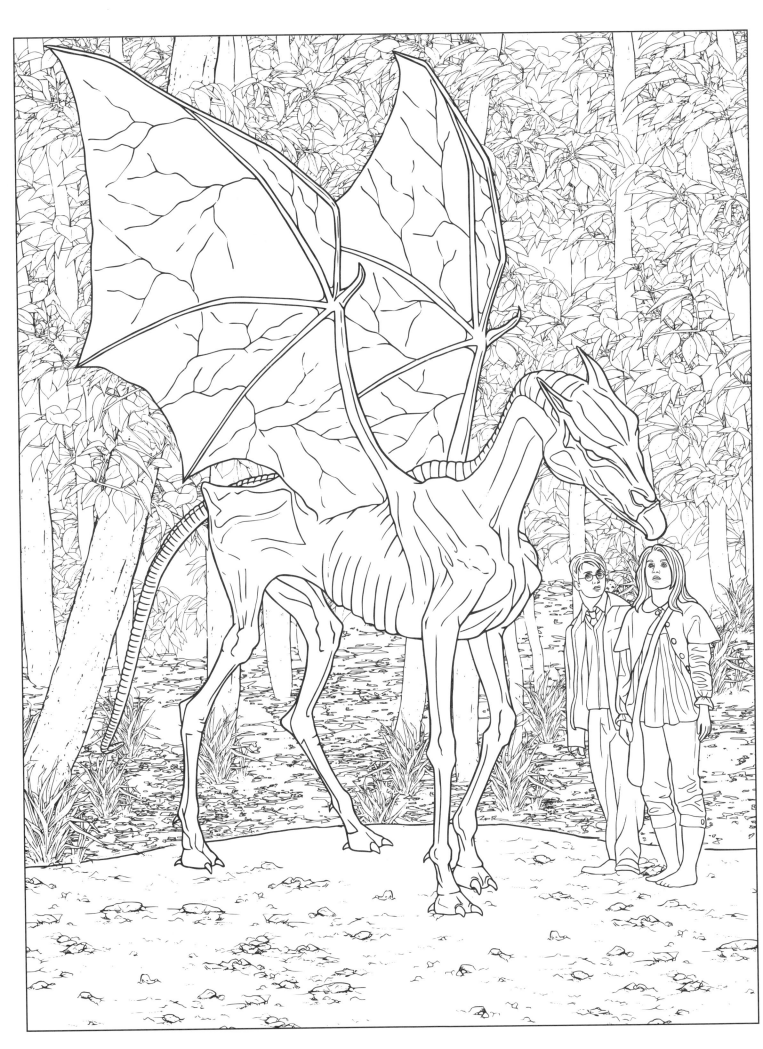

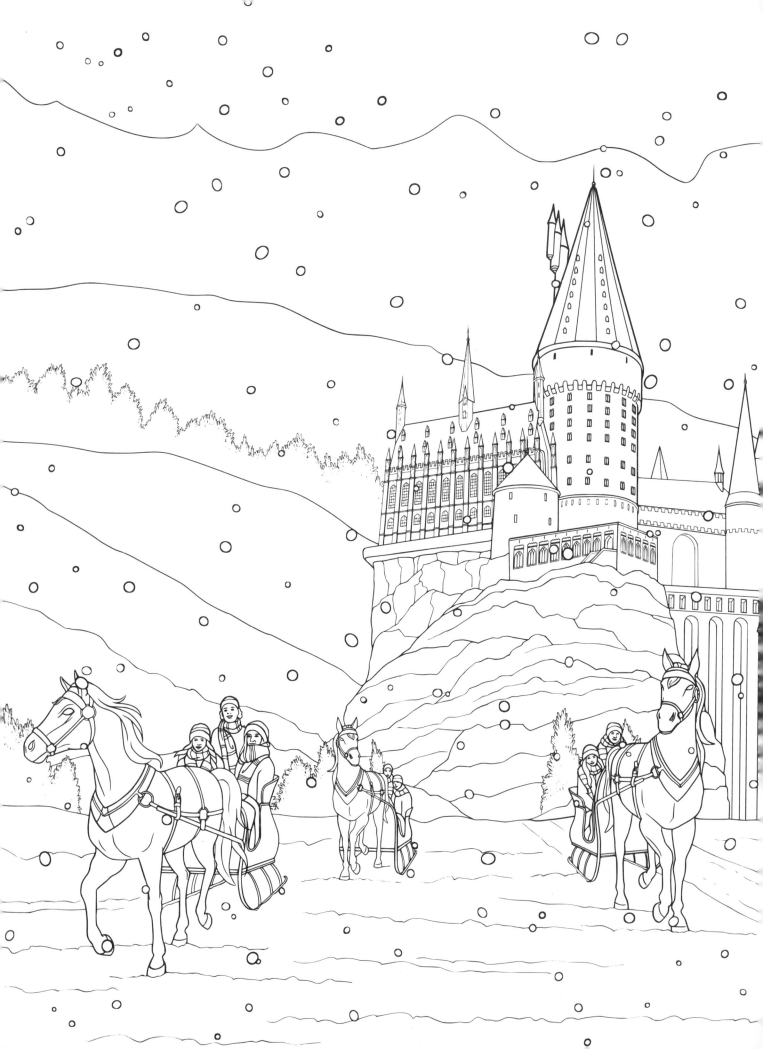

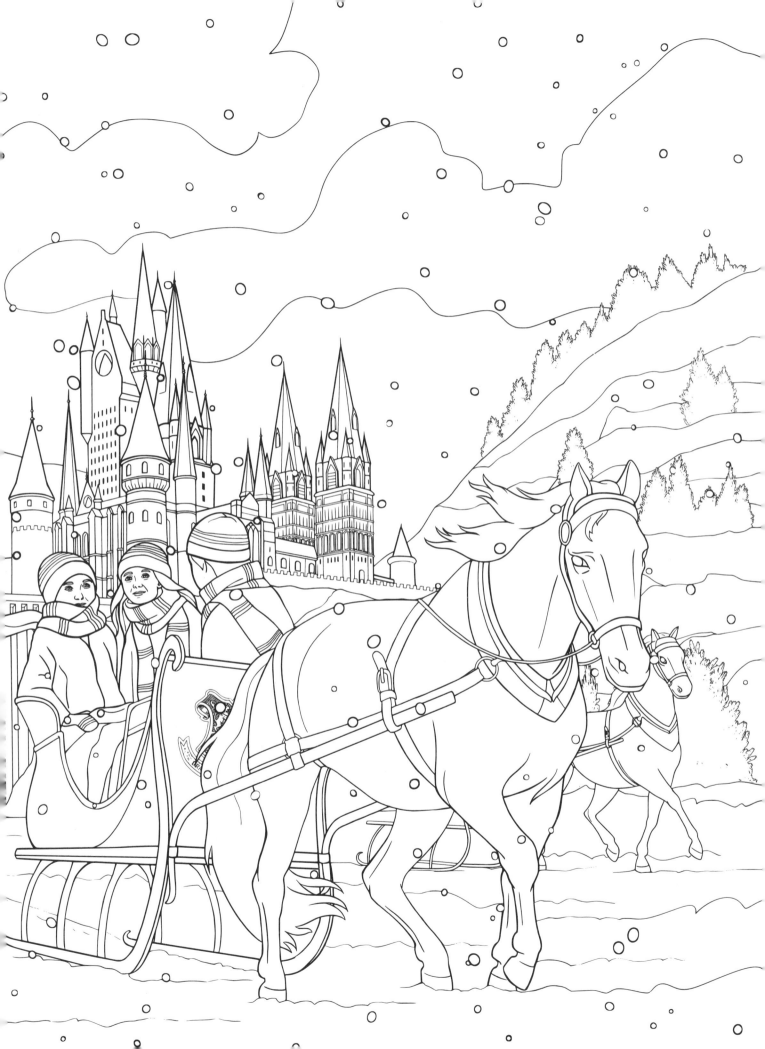

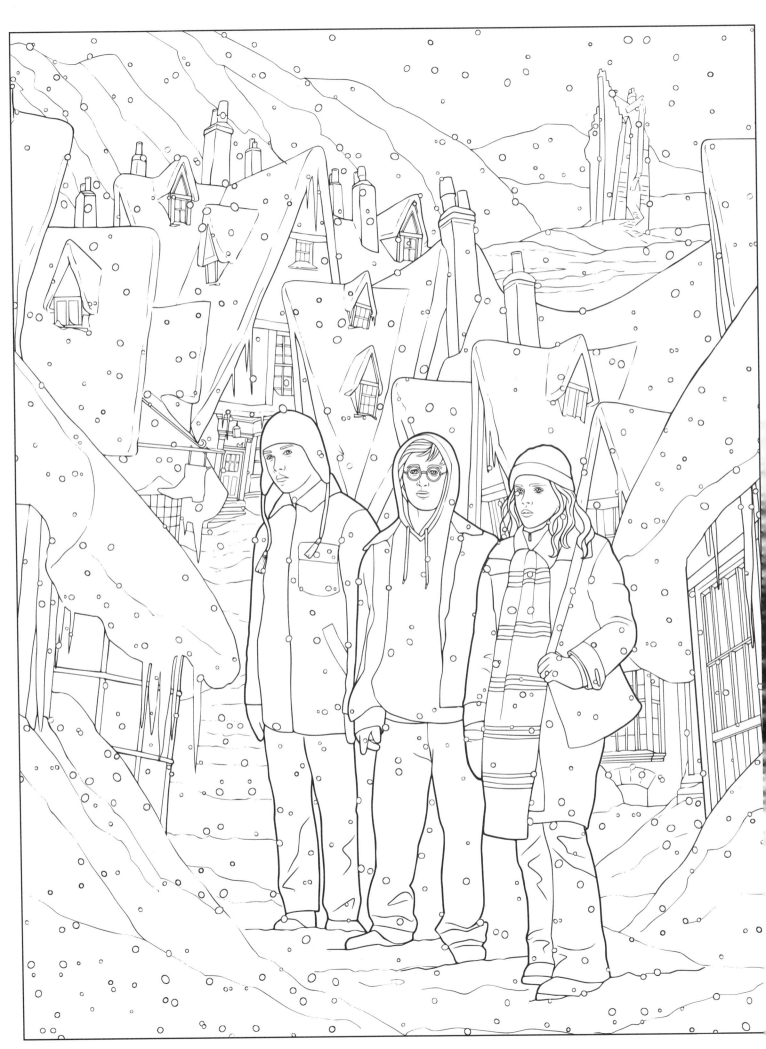

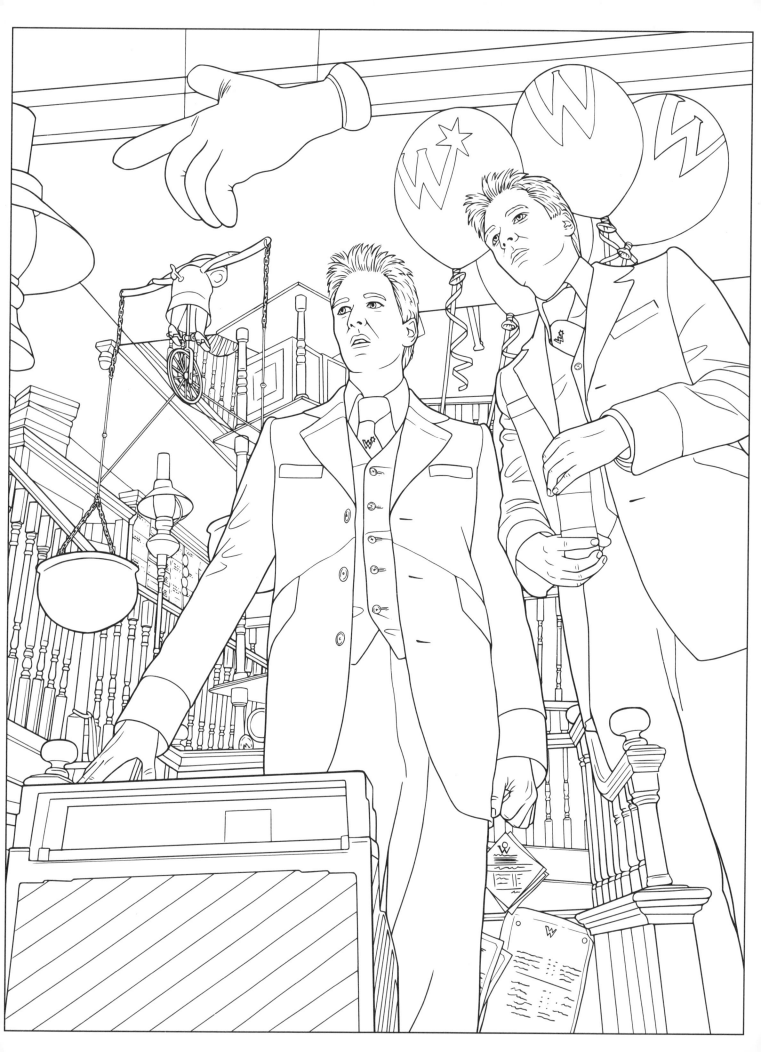

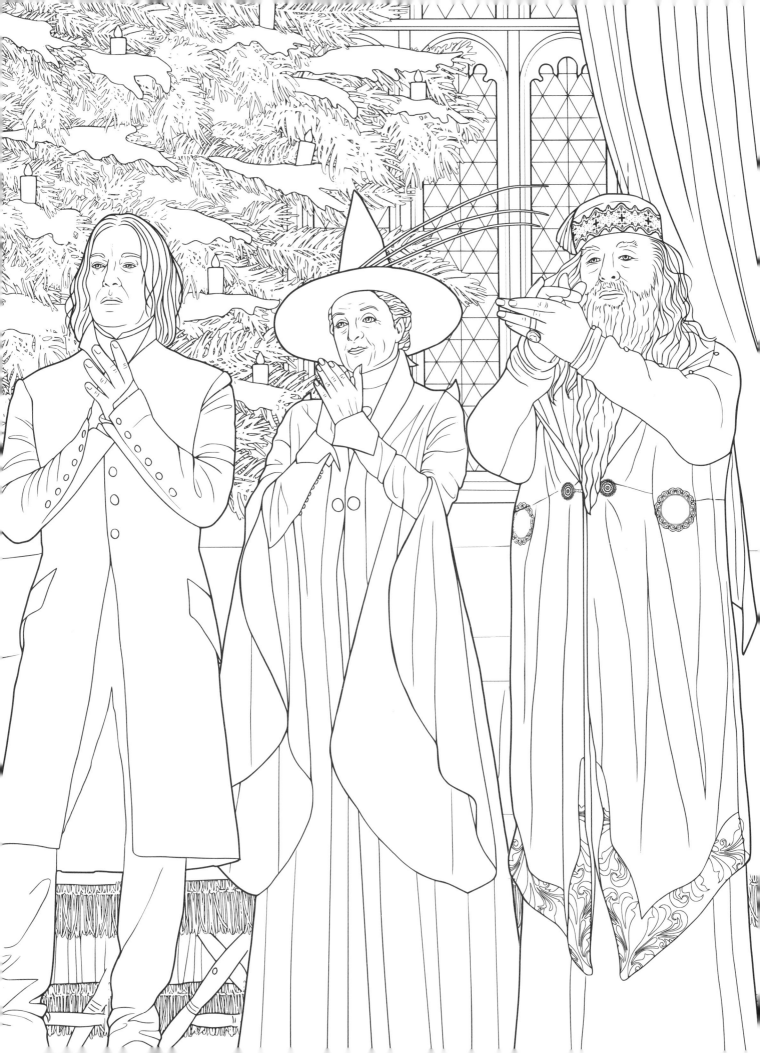

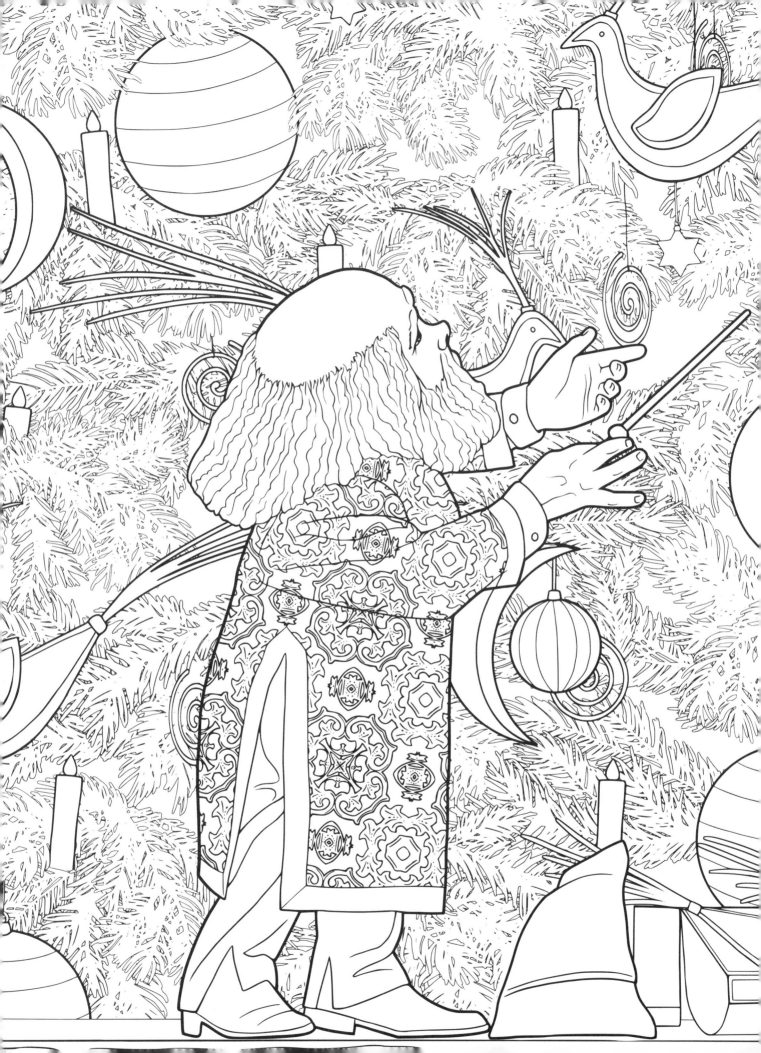

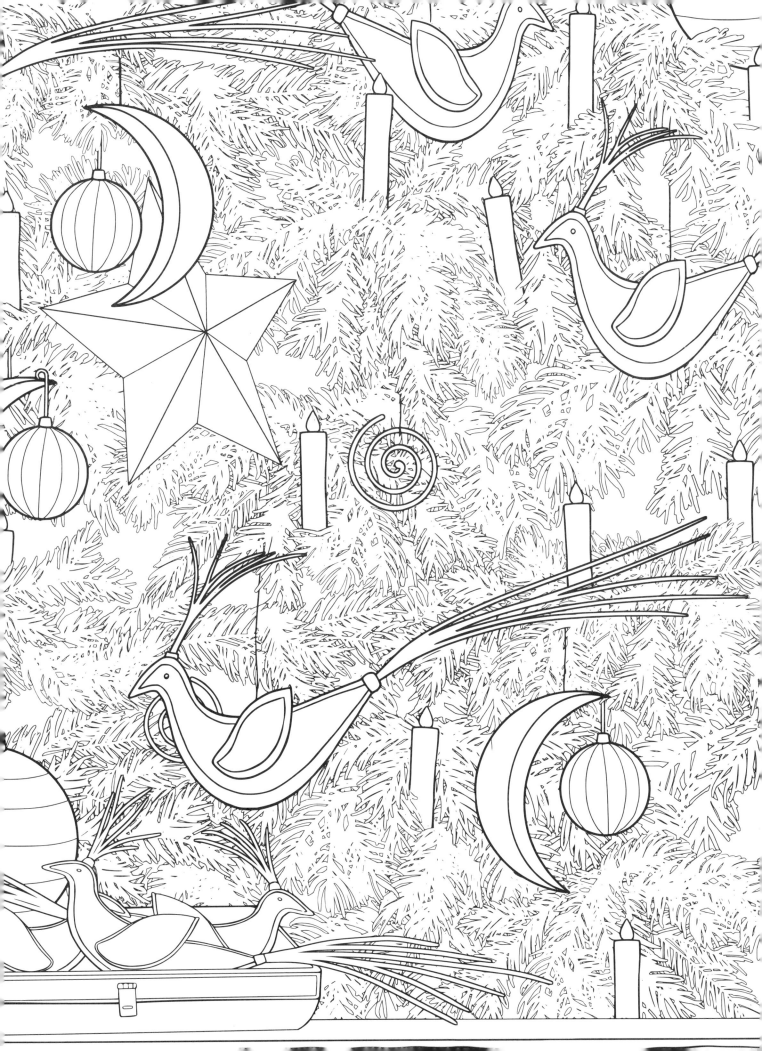

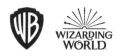

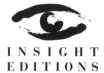

PO Box 3088
San Rafael, CA 94912
www.insighteditions.com

Find us on Facebook: www.facebook.com/InsightEditions
Follow us on Twitter: @insighteditions

Library of Congress Cataloging-in-Publication Data available.

ISBN: 979-8-88663-043-5

Publisher: Raoul Goff
VP of Licensing and Partnerships: Vanessa Lopez
VP of Creative: Chrissy Kwasnik
VP of Manufacturing: Alix Nicholaeff
VP, Editorial Director: Vicki Jaeger
Senior Designer: Judy Wiatrek Trum
Editorial Assistant: Sami Alvarado
Production Editor: Michael Hylton
Production Associate: Tiffani Patterson
Senior Production Manager, Subsidiary Rights: Lina s Palma-Temena

Illustrations by Paula Rozelle Hanback

Edited by Scott Nybakken

ROOTS of PEACE   REPLANTED PAPER

Insight Editions, in association with Roots of Peace, will plant two trees for each
tree used in the manufacturing of this book. Roots of Peace is an internationally
renowned humanitarian organization dedicated to eradicating land mines worldwide
and converting war-torn lands into productive farms and wildlife habitats. Roots of
Peace will plant two million fruit and nut trees in Afghanistan and provide farmers
there with the skills and support necessary for sustainable land use.

Manufactured in China by Insight Editions

10 9 8 7 6 5 4 3